FREEDOM OF RELIGION DECISIONS OF THE UNITED STATES SUPREME COURT

MAUREEN HARRISON & STEVE GILBERT
EDITORS

FIRST AMENDMENT DECISIONS SERIES

EXCELLENT BOOKS
SAN DIEGO, CALIFORNIA

EXCELLENT BOOKS
Post Office Box 927105
San Diego, CA 92192-7105

Publisher's Cataloging in Publication Data

Freedom of Religion Decisions of the United States Supreme Court/
  Maureen Harrison, Steve Gilbert, editors.
  p. cm. - (First Amendment Decisions Series)
Bibliography: p.
Includes Index.
1. Freedom of Religion - United States - Cases.
2. United States. Supreme Court.
I. Title. II. Harrison, Maureen. III. Gilbert, Steve.
IV. Series: First Amendment Decisions.
KF4783.A7 H24 1996   LC 96-83103
342.0852-dc20
ISBN 1-880780-11-9

INTRODUCTION

Freedom of Religion was first in the Bill of Rights because it was first in the forefathers' minds; it was set forth in absolute terms, and its strength is its rigidity.
- Justice Robert Jackson

You will not find the word *God* in the U.S. Constitution. Yet their personal relationship to a Supreme Being must have been very much on the minds of the Founding Fathers as guarantees to all Americans of the right to worship free of Government interference was written, not once but twice, into the Constitution's First Amendment.

The First Amendment's two Religion Clauses are in total only sixteen words in length: *Congress shall make no law respecting an establishment of religion, or prohibiting the free exercise thereof.*

The Establishment Clause: *Congress shall make no law respecting an establishment of religion* forbids the Federal Government from either establishing any official national religion or showing any preference to one religion over another. In the 1947 *Everson* Decision (see page 33) the Supreme Court extended the Establishment Clause's prohibitions, via the Fourteenth Amendment, to state and local governments.

The Free Exercise Clause: *Congress shall make no law prohibiting the free exercise [of religion]* forbids the Federal Government's interference with the rights of individual Americans to practice the religion of their choice. In the 1940 *Cantwell* Decision (see page 19) the Supreme Court extended the Free Exercise Clause's prohibitions, via the Fourteenth Amendment, to state and local governments.

Taken together the First Amendment's Establishment and Free Exercise Clauses created what Thomas Jefferson

called *a wall of separation between Church and State.*
The Religion Clauses of the Constitution's First Amendment are the Founding Father's guarantee that the wall of separation between Church and State will not be breached by the Federal Government. The Supreme Court, through the Due Process Clause of the Constitution's Fourteenth Amendment, applies these same First Amendment protections against interference in matters of religion by state and local governments. The final arbiter of the meaning of the First Amendment's Establishment and Free Exercise Clauses, given this role by Article Three of the Constitution, is the United States Supreme Court.

In *Freedom of Religion Decisions* we have selected and edited eighteen landmark First Amendment Establishment and Free Exercise cases that clearly illustrate the importance of Jefferson's wall of separation between Church and State.

Judge Learned Hand wrote: "The language of the law must not be foreign to the ears of those who are to obey it." The eighteen *Freedom of Religion Decisions* presented in this book are carefully edited versions of the official texts issued by the Supreme Court in *United States Reports*. We, as editors, have made every effort to replace esoteric legalese with plain English without damaging the original decisions. Edited out are long alpha-numeric legal citations and wordy wrangles over points of procedure. Edited in are definitions (*writ of habeas corpus* = an order from a judge to bring a person to court), translations (*certiorari* = the decision of the Court to review a case), identifications (Appellant = Pierce), Appellee = Society of Sisters), and explanations (where the case originated, how it got to the court, what the issues were, and who the parties were).

You will find in this book the majority opinion of the Court as expressed by the Justice chosen to speak for the

Court. Preceding each edited decision, we note where the complete decision can be found. The bibliography provides a list of further readings on the cases and the Court. Also included for the reader's reference is a complete copy of the United States Constitution, to which every decision refers.

Every year over five thousand requests for review of lower court decisions are received by the Court. Requests, called petitions for *certiorari*, come to the Court from the losing side in Federal Appeals or State Supreme Courts. Four of the nine Justices must agree to a review. Only four hundred cases are accepted each year. Once accepted, written arguments, called briefs, pro and con, are submitted to the Court by both the petitioner, the side appealing the lower court decision against them, and the respondent, the side defending the lower court decision in their favor. Interested parties, called *amici curiae* [friends of the Court], may be permitted to file their own briefs in support of either side. After briefs are submitted to and reviewed by the Justices, public oral arguments are heard by the Court. Lawyers for the petitioner and respondent are allowed thirty minutes to make their case before the Justices. The Justices, at their discretion, may interrupt at any time to require further explanations, to pose hypothetical questions, or make observations.

Twice a week, on Wednesday and Friday, the Justices meet alone in conference to discuss each case and to vote on the outcome. They may affirm [uphold] or reverse [change the outcome of], in whole or in part, the decisions of the lower courts from which these appeals have come. One Justice, voting in the majority, will be selected to write the majority opinion. In rare instances the Court will issue its decision *per curiam* [by the Court majority without attribution of authorship]. Justices may join in the majority opinion, write their own concurring opinion, write their own dissenting opinion, or join in another's concurrence or dissent. Drafts of the majority, concurring, and dissenting opinions circulate among the Justices for their comments. Opinions are redrafted and recirculated until a consensus is reached and a carefully worded decision is announced. It is the majority decision that stands as the law of the land.

The representative selection of Supreme Court cases you will find in *Freedom of Religion Decisions* are, on their face, solely about the rights of individual Americans: Protestants, Catholics, Jews, Mormons, and Jehovah's Witnesses; and single issues: school prayer, religious rituals, education. These decisions are, in fact, about the rights of all religious sects and the protection of all their practitioners. These decisions, creating legal precedents that have endured for generations, have fundamentally altered the relationships of Americans to their institutions and to each other. They represent the great and continuing controversies of our times and are presented here for the first time to the general non-legal reader in plain English.

In 1960 John F. Kennedy, addressing a gathering of Ministers, said: *I believe in an America where the separation of church and state is absolute . . . where no church or church school is granted any public funds or political preference. . . . I believe in an America that is officially neither Catholic, Protestant, nor Jewish . . . where no religious body seeks to impose its will directly or indirectly upon the general populace or the public acts of its officials - and where religious liberty is so indivisible that an act against one church is treated as an act against all.*

We hope that readers of *Freedom of Religion Decisions* will find within these pages the reasons and rationales for the belief, in common with President Kennedy's own, that religious liberty in America should always be absolute and indivisible.

M.H. & S.G.

TABLE OF CONTENTS

[The law provides] that plural marriages shall not be allowed. Can a man excuse his practices to the contrary because of his religious belief? To permit this would be to make the professed doctrines of religious belief superior to the law of the land. - Chief Justice Morrison Waite
Reynolds v. United States

The fundamental theory of liberty upon which all governments in this Union repose excludes any general power of the State to standardize its children by forcing them to accept instruction from public teachers only.
- Justice James McReynolds
Pierce v. Society of Sisters

The essential characteristic of [religious liberty] is that under [its] shield many types of life, character, opinion and belief can develop unmolested and unobstructed. Nowhere is this shield more necessary than in our own country for a people composed of many races and of many creeds. - Justice Owen Roberts
Cantwell v. Connecticut

Public Money For Religious Purposes
33

The First Amendment has erected a wall between church and state. That wall must be kept high and impregnable. We could not approve the slightest breach.
- Justice Hugo Black
Everson v. Ewing Board of Education

Early Release Time For Religious Instruction
43

We cannot read into the Bill of Rights a philosophy of hostility to religion.   - Justice William O. Douglas
Zorach v. Clauson

School Prayer
51

It has been argued that to apply the Constitution in such a way as to prohibit state laws respecting an establishment of religious services in public schools is to indicate a hostility toward religion or toward prayer. Nothing, of course, could be more wrong.   - Justice Hugo Black
Engel v. Vitale

Bible Reading In The Public Schools
63

In the relationship between man and religion, the State is firmly committed to a position of neutrality.
- Justice Tom Clark
Abington Schools v. Schempp
Murray v. Curlett

The "Monkey" Law
73

The First Amendment mandates government neutrality between religion and religion, and between religion and non-religion. - Justice Abe Fortas
Epperson v. Arkansas

Tax Exemptions For Church Property
85

The hazards of churches supporting government are hardly less in their potential than the hazards of government supporting churches; each relationship carries some involvement rather than the desired insulation and separation. - Chief Justice Warren Burger
Walz v. New York Tax Commission

Taxpayer Support Of Religious Schools
95

Under our system the choice has been made that government is to be entirely excluded from the area of religious instruction and churches excluded from the affairs of government. - Chief Justice Warren Burger
Lemon v. Kurtzman
Robinson v. DiCenso

Compulsory Education Of The Amish
103

A way of life, however virtuous and admirable, may not be interposed as a barrier to reasonable state regulation of education if is based on purely secular considerations; to have the protection of the Religion Clauses, the claims must be rooted in religious belief.
- Chief Justice Warren Burger
Wisconsin v. Yoder

The "Ten Commandments" Act
113

The pre-eminent purpose for posting the Ten Command-
ments on schoolroom walls is plainly religious in nature.
The Ten Commandments are undeniably a sacred text in
the Jewish and Christian faiths and no legislative recita-
tion of a supposed secular purpose can blind us to that
fact. - *Per Curiam* [by the Court]
Stone v. Graham

The Creche Case
119

[T]he purpose of the Establishment and Free Exercise
Clauses of the First Amendment is "to prevent, as far as
possible, the intrusion of either [the Church or the State]
into the precincts of the other."
- Chief Justice Warren Burger
Lynch v. Donnelly

Islamic Prayers In Prison
129

[T]he very stringent requirements as to the time at which
[the Islamic prayer service] may be held make it extraor-
dinarily difficult for prison officials to assure that every
Muslim prisoner is able to attend that service.
- Chief Justice William Rehnquist
O'Lone v. Shabazz

Distribution Of Religious Literature
137

[T]he resolution at issue in this case reaches the universe
of expressive activity, and, by prohibiting all *protected ex-*
pression, purports to create a virtual "First Amendment
Free Zone." - Justice Sandra Day O'Connor
LAX v. Jews For Jesus

This book is dedicated with love to our Aunt Catherine.

No man shall be compelled to frequent or support any religious worship, place, or ministry, nor shall otherwise suffer on account of his religious opinions or belief; but all men shall be free to profess, and by argument to maintain, their opinions in matters of religion.

- Thomas Jefferson

Mormon Polygamy
Reynolds v. United States

Every person having a husband or wife living, who marries another, whether married or single, in a Territory, or other place over which the United States have exclusive jurisdiction, is guilty of bigamy.

-The Federal Anti-Polygamy Law

In the mid- to late 1800's polygamy, a male being married at the same time to more than one female, was endorsed, as a part of their religious beliefs by the leaders, and became the accepted practice of the followers, of the Church of Jesus Christ of Latter Day Saints, commonly know as the Mormons. George Reynolds, a Mormon, living in the Utah Territory in the 1870's, and acting in accordance with his faith, was married to both Mary Anne Tuddenham and Amelia Jane Schofield.

The practice of polygamy was against the law in all U.S. States and Territories. Utah had become a Territory in 1848. Reynolds was indicted for a violation of the Federal Anti-Polygamy Law and tried for bigamy. Reynolds, asserting that it was the religious duty of male members of the Mormon Church to practice polygamy, a practice he believed to be a right protected in the Utah Territory by the United States Constitution's First Amendment, pled not guilty. The Judge instructed the jury, from which all persons professing a belief in or tolerance of polygamy had been excluded, that Reynold's religious beliefs did not excuse him from deliberately violating the law. The jury found him guilty. The Utah Supreme Court rejected Reynold's appeal for a reversal and Reynolds appealed to the United States Supreme Court.

The 9-0 decision of the Court was announced on May 5, 1879 by Chief Justice Morrison Waite.

THE REYNOLDS COURT

Chief Justice Morrison Waite
Appointed Chief Justice by President Grant
Served 1874 - 1888

Associate Justice Nathan Clifford
Appointed by President Buchanan
Served 1858 -1881

Associate Justice Noah Swayne
Appointed by President Lincoln
Served 1862 - 1881

Associate Justice Samuel Miller
Appointed by President Lincoln
Served 1862 - 1890

Associate Justice Stephen Field
Appointed by President Lincoln
Served 1863 - 1897

Associate Justice William Strong
Appointed by President Grant
Served 1870 - 1880

Associate Justice Joseph Bradley
Appointed by President Grant
Served 1870 - 1892

Associate Justice Ward Hunt
Appointed by President Grant
Served 1873 - 1882

Associate Justice John Marshall Harlan
Appointed by President Hayes
Served 1877 - 1911

The unedited text of *Reynolds v. United States* can be found on page 145, volume 98 of *United States Reports.*

REYNOLDS v. UNITED STATES
May 5, 1879

CHIEF JUSTICE WAITE: "This is an indictment [charge] found in the District Court for the . . . Territory of Utah, charging George Reynolds with bigamy, in violation of [the Anti-Polygamy Section] of the Revised Statutes, which . . . is as follows:

> 'Every person having a husband or wife living, who marries another, whether married or single, in a Territory, or other place over which the United States have exclusive jurisdiction, is guilty of bigamy, and shall by punished by a fine of not more than $500, and by imprisonment for a term of not more than five years.'"

The assignments of error [arguments], when grouped, present the following questions:

> . . . . Should the accused have been acquitted if he married the second time, because he believed it to be his religious duty?

> Did the court err in that part of the charge which directed the attention of the jury to the consequences of polygamy?

These questions will be considered in their order.

. . . . As to the defense of religious belief or duty:

On the trial, the plaintiff in error, the accused [Reynolds], proved that at the time of his alleged second marriage he was, and for many years before had been, a member of the Church of Jesus Christ of Latter-Day Saints, commonly called the Mormon Church, and a believer in its doctrines; that it was an accepted doctrine of that church "that it was the duty of male members of said church, circumstances permitting, to practice polygamy; . . . that this duty was enjoined [required] by different books which the members of said church believed to be of divine origin, and among others the Holy Bible, and also that the members of the church believed that the practice of polygamy was directly enjoined upon the male members thereof by the Almighty God, in a revelation to Joseph Smith, the founder and prophet of said church; that the failing or refusing to practice polygamy by such male members of said church, when circumstances would admit, would be punished, and that the penalty for such failure and refusal would be damnation in the life to come." He also proved "that he had received permission from the recognized authorities in said church to enter into polygamous marriage; . . . that Daniel H. Wells, one having authority in said church to perform the marriage ceremony, married the said defendant on or about the time the crime is alleged to have been committed, to some woman by the name of Schofield, and that such marriage ceremony was performed under and pursuant to the doctrines of said church."

Upon this proof he asked the court to instruct the jury that if they found from the evidence that he "was married as charged - if he was married - in pursuance of and in conformity with what he believed at the time to be a religious duty, that the verdict must be 'not guilty'." This request was refused, and the court did charge "that there must have been a criminal intent, but that if the defendant, under the influence of a religious belief that it was right - under an inspiration, if you please, that it was right

- deliberately married a second time, having a first wife living, the want of consciousness of evil intent - the want of understanding on his part that he was committing a crime - did not excuse him; but the law inexorably in such case implies the criminal intent."

Upon this charge and refusal to charge the question is raised, whether religious belief can be accepted as a justification of an overt act made criminal by the law of the land. The inquiry is not as to the power of Congress to prescribe criminal laws for the Territories, but as to the guilt of one who knowingly violates a law which has been properly enacted, if he entertains a religious belief that the law is wrong.

Congress cannot pass a law for the government of the Territories which shall prohibit the free exercise of religion. The first amendment to the constitution expressly forbids such legislation. Religious freedom is guaranteed everywhere throughout the United States, so far as congressional interference is concerned. The question to be determined is, whether the law now under consideration comes within this prohibition.

The word "religion" is not defined in the Constitution. We must go elsewhere, therefore, to ascertain its meaning, and nowhere more appropriately, we think, than to the history of the times in the midst of which the provision was adopted. The precise point of the inquiry is, what is the religious freedom which has been guaranteed.

Before the adoption of the Constitution, attempts were made in some of the colonies and States to legislate not only in respect to the establishment of religion, but in respect to its doctrines and precepts as well. The people were taxed, against their will, for the support of religion, and sometimes for the support of particular sects to whose tenets they could not and did not subscribe. Punishments were prescribed for a failure to attend upon public worship, and sometimes for entertaining heretical opinions. The controversy upon this general subject was animated in many of the States, but seemed at last to culminate in Virginia. In 1784, the House of Delegates of that State having under consideration "a bill establishing provision for teachers of the Christian religion," postponed it until the next session, and directed that the bill should be published and distributed, and that the people be requested "to signify their opinion respecting the adoption of such a bill at the next session of assembly."

This brought out a determined opposition. Amongst others, Mr. Madison prepared a "Memorial and Remonstrance," which was widely circulated and signed, and in which he demonstrated "that religion, or the duty we owe the Creator," was not within the cognizance of civil government. At the next session the proposed bill was not only defeated, but another, "for establishing religious freedom," drafted by Mr. Jefferson, was passed. In the preamble of this act religious freedom is defined; and after a recital "that to suffer the civil magistrate to intrude his powers into the field of opinion, and to restrain the profession or propagation of principles on supposition of their ill tendency, is a dangerous fallacy which at once destroys all religious liberty," it is declared "that it is time enough for the rightful purposes of civil government for its officers to interfere when principles break out into overt acts against peace and good order." In these two sentences is found the true distinction between what properly belongs to the church and what to the State.

In a little more than a year after the passage of this statute the convention met which prepared the Constitution
of the United States. Of this convention Mr. Jefferson
was not a member, he being then absent as minister to
France. As soon as he saw the draft of the Constitution
proposed for adoption, he, in a letter to a friend, expressed his disappointment at the absence of an express
declaration insuring the freedom of religion, but was willing to accept it as it was, trusting that the good sense and
honest intentions of the people would bring about the
necessary alterations. Five of the States, while adopting
the Constitution, proposed amendments. Three - New
Hampshire, New York, and Virginia - included in one
form or another a declaration of religious freedom in the
changes they desired to have made, as did also North
Carolina, where the convention at first declined to ratify
the Constitution until the proposed amendments were acted upon. Accordingly, at the first session of the first Congress the amendment now under consideration was proposed with others by Mr. Madison. It met the views of
the advocates of religious freedom, and was adopted. . . .
Congress was deprived of all legislative power over mere
opinion, but was left free to reach actions which were in
violation of social duties or subversive of good order.

Polygamy has always been odious among the northern and
western nations of Europe, and, until the establishment of
the Mormon Church, was almost exclusively a feature of
the life of Asiatic and of African people. At common law
[customary law], the second marriage was always void, and
from the earliest history of England polygamy has been
treated as an offense against society. After the establishment of the ecclesiastical courts, and until the time of
James I, it was punished through the instrumentality of
those tribunals, not merely because ecclesiastical rights

had been violated, but because upon the separation of the ecclesiastical courts from the civil the ecclesiastical were supposed to be the most appropriate for the trial of matrimonial causes and offenses against the rights of marriage, just as they were for testamentary causes and the settlement of the estates of deceased persons.

By the statute of James I, the offense, if committed in England or Wales, was made punishable in the civil courts, and the penalty was death. As this statute was limited in its operation to England and Wales, it was at a very early period re-enacted, generally with some modifications, in all the colonies. In connection with the case we are now considering, it is a significant fact that on the eighth of December, 1788, after the passage of the act establishing religious freedom, and after the convention of Virginia had recommended as an amendment to the Constitution of the United States the declaration in a bill of rights that "all men have an equal, natural, and unalienable right to the free exercise of religion, according to the dictates of conscience," the legislature of that State substantially enacted the statute of James I, death penalty included, because, as recited in the preamble, "it hath been doubted whether bigamy or polygamy be punishable by the laws of this Commonwealth." From that day to this we think it may safely be said there never has been a time in any State of the Union when polygamy has not been an offense against society, cognizable by the civil courts and punishable with more or less severity. In the face of all this evidence, it is impossible to believe that the constitutional guaranty of religious freedom was intended to prohibit legislation in respect to this most important feature of social life. Marriage, while from its very nature a sacred obligation, is nevertheless, in most civilized nations, a civil contract, and usually regulated by law. Upon it society may be said to be built, and out of its fruits spring social relations and social obligations and duties, with which government is necessarily required to deal. . . . An exceptional colony of polygamists under an exceptional leadership may sometimes exist for a time without appearing to disturb the social condition of the people who surround it; but there cannot be a doubt that, unless restricted by some form of constitution, it is within the legitimate scope of the power of every civil government to determine whether polygamy or monogamy shall be the law of social life under its dominion.

In our opinion, the statute immediately under consideration is within the legislative power of Congress. It is constitutional and valid as prescribing a rule of action for all those residing in the Territories, and in places over which the United States have exclusive control. This being so, the only question which remains is, whether those who make polygamy a part of their religion are excepted from the operation of the statute. If they are, then those who do not make polygamy a part of their religious belief may be found guilty and punished, while those who do, must be acquitted and go free. This would be introducing a new element into criminal law. Laws are made for the government of actions, and while they cannot interfere with mere religious belief and opinions, they may with practices. Suppose one believed that human sacrifices were a necessary part of religious worship, would it be seriously contended that the civil government under which he lived could not interfere to prevent a sacrifice? Or if a wife religiously believed it was her duty to burn herself upon the funeral pile of her dead husband, would it be beyond the power of the civil government to prevent her carrying her belief into practice?

So here, as a law of the organization of society under the exclusive dominion of the United States, it is provided that plural marriages shall not be allowed. Can a man excuse his practices to the contrary because of his religious belief? To permit this would be to make the professed doctrines of religious belief superior to the law of the land, and in effect to permit every citizen to become a law unto himself. Government could exist only in name under such circumstances.

A criminal intent is generally an element of crime, but every man is presumed to intend the necessary and legitimate consequences of what he knowingly does. Here the accused knew he had been once married, and that his first wife was living. He also knew that his second marriage was forbidden by law. When, therefore, he married the second time, he is presumed to have intended to break the law. And the breaking of the law is the crime. Every act necessary to constitute the crime was knowingly done, and the crime was therefore knowingly committed. Ignorance of a fact may sometimes be taken as evidence of a want of criminal intent, but not ignorance of the law. The only defense of the accused in this case is his belief that the law ought not to have been enacted. It matters not that his belief was a part of his professed religion: it was still belief, and belief only.

.... As to that part of the charge which directed the attention of the jury to the consequences of polygamy:

The passage complained of is as follows: "I think it not improper, in the discharge of your duties in this case, that you should consider what are to be the consequences to the innocent victims of this delusion. As this contest goes on, they multiply, and there are pure-minded women and there are innocent children - innocent in a sense even beyond the degree of the innocence of childhood itself. These are to be the sufferers; and as jurors fail to do their duty, and as these cases come up in the Territory of Utah, just so do these victims multiply and spread themselves over the land."

While every appeal by the court to the passions or the prejudices of a jury should be promptly rebuked, and while it is the imperative duty of a reviewing court to take care that wrong is not done in this way, we see no just cause for complaint in this case. Congress, in 1862, saw fit to make bigamy a crime in the Territories. This was done because of the evil consequences that were supposed to flow from plural marriages. All the court did was to call the attention of the jury to the peculiar character of the crime for which the accused was on trial, and to remind them of the duty they had to perform. There was no appeal to the passions, no instigation of prejudice. Upon the showing made by the accused himself, he was guilty of a violation of the law under which he had been indicted; and the effort of the court seems to have been not to withdraw the minds of the jury from the issue to be tried, but to bring them to it; not to make them partial, but to keep them impartial.

Upon a careful consideration of the whole case, we are satisfied that no error was committed by the court below.

Judgment affirmed.

The Right To Attend A Parochial School
Pierce v. Society Of Sisters

Any parent, guardian, or other person having control of a child between eight and sixteen years who shall fail or neglect to send such child to a public school shall be guilty of a misdemeanor.

- Oregon's Compulsory Public Education Law

On November 7, 1922 the voters of the State of Oregon passed a ballot initiative called the Compulsory Public Education Law. This law required that every parent, guardian, or other person having control of a child between the ages of eight and sixteen years send that child, under penalty of law, to a public school. The Compulsory Public Education Law, which was to go into effect on September 1, 1926, would have the effect of closing all of Oregon's private parochial schools.

The Society of Sisters was formed in Oregon in 1880 to care for and educate orphans. The Society, affiliated with the Catholic Church, operated private parochial schools for elementary and secondary instruction of both orphans under their care and the children of parents and guardians who chose to send their children to this private religious institution. Compliance with the Compulsory Public Education Law would have shut down the Society's schools.

The Society, asserting that the State had no power to force parents to send their children to public school against their will, sued Governor Pierce of Oregon to stop the enforcement of the Compulsory Public Education Law. A Federal District Court ruled that Oregon's law violated the United States Constitution. Oregon appealed for a reversal to the United States Supreme Court.

Oral arguments were heard on March 16, 1925 and on June 1, 1925 the 9-0 decision of the Court was announced by Associate Justice James McReynolds.

THE SOCIETY OF SISTERS COURT

Chief Justice William Howard Taft
Appointed Chief Justice by President Hoover
Served 1930 - 1941

Associate Justice Oliver Wendell Holmes, Jr.
Appointed by President Theodore Roosevelt
Served 1902 - 1932

Associate Justice Willis Van Devanter
Appointed by President Taft
Served 1910 - 1937

Associate Justice James McReynolds
Appointed by President Wilson
Served 1914 - 1941

Associate Justice Louis Brandeis
Appointed by President Wilson
Served 1916 - 1939

Associate Justice George Sutherland
Appointed by President Harding
Served 1922 - 1938

Associate Justice Pierce Butler
Appointed by President Harding
Served 1922 - 1939

Associate Justice Edward Sanford
Appointed by President Harding
Served 1923 - 1930

Associate Justice Harlan Fiske Stone
Appointed by President Coolidge
Served 1925 - 1946

The unedited text of *Pierce v. Society of Sisters* can be found on page 510, volume 268 of *United States Reports.*

PIERCE v. SOCIETY OF SISTERS
June 1, 1925

JUSTICE McREYNOLDS: These appeals are from decrees [of the U.S. District Court], which granted preliminary orders restraining appellants [the Governor of Ore-
gon] from threatening or attempting to enforce the
[State's] Compulsory Education Act adopted November 7,
1922, under the initiative provision of her Constitution
by the voters of Oregon. . . .

The challenged Act, effective September 1, 1926, requires
every parent, guardian or other person having control or
charge or custody of a child between eight and sixteen
years to send him "to a public school for the period of
time a public school shall be held during the current year"
in the district where the child resides; and failure so to do
is declared a misdemeanor [lesser offense]. . . . The mani-
fest purpose is to compel general attendance at public
schools by . . . children, between eight and sixteen, who
have not completed the eighth grade. . . .

Appellee, the Society of Sisters, is an Oregon corporation,
organized in 1880, with power to care for orphans, educate and instruct the youth, establish and maintain acade-
mies or schools, and acquire necessary real and personal
property. It has long devoted its property and effort to
the secular and religious education and care of children,
and has acquired the valuable good will of many parents
and guardians. It conducts interdependent primary and
high schools and junior colleges, and maintains orphanages
for the custody and control of children between eight and
sixteen. In its primary schools many children between
those ages are taught the subjects usually pursued in Oregon public schools during the first eight years. Systematic

religious instruction and moral training according to the tenets of the Roman Catholic Church are also regularly provided. All courses of study, both temporal and religious, contemplate continuity of training under [the Society]'s charge; the primary schools are essential to the system and the most profitable. It owns valuable buildings, especially constructed and equipped for school purposes. The business is remunerative - the annual income from primary schools exceeds thirty thousand dollars - and the successful conduct of this requires long time contracts with teachers and parents. The Compulsory Education Act of 1922 has already caused the withdrawal from its schools of children who would otherwise continue, and their income has steadily declined. The appellants, public officers, have proclaimed their purpose strictly to enforce the statute.

After setting out the above facts the Society's bill alleges that the enactment conflicts with the right of parents to choose schools where their children will receive appropriate mental and religious training, the right of the child to influence the parents' choice of a school, the right of schools and teachers therein to engage in a useful business or profession, and is accordingly repugnant to the Constitution and void. And, further, that unless enforcement of the measure is enjoined [prohibited] the corporation's business and property will suffer irreparable injury.

. . . . [A]fter proper notices [the cause was] heard by three [U.S. District] judges on motions for preliminary injunctions [court orders stopping an action] upon the specifically alleged facts. The court ruled that the Fourteenth Amendment guaranteed appellees against the deprivation of their property without due process of law consequent upon the unlawful interference by appellants with the free choice of patrons, present and prospective. It declared the right to conduct schools was property and that parents and guardians, as a part of their liberty, might direct the education of children by selecting reputable teachers and places. Also, that these schools were not unfit or harmful to the public, and that enforcement of the challenged statute would unlawfully deprive them of patronage and thereby destroy their owners' business and property. Finally, that the threats to enforce the Act would continue to cause irreparable injury; and the suits were not premature.

No question is raised concerning the power of the State reasonably to regulate all schools, to inspect, supervise and examine them, their teachers and pupils; to require that all children of proper age attend some school, that teachers shall be of good moral character and patriotic disposition, that certain studies plainly essential to good citizenship must be taught, and that nothing be taught which is manifestly inimical to the public welfare.

The inevitable practical result of enforcing the Act under consideration would be destruction of [the Society's] primary schools, and perhaps all other private primary schools for normal children within the State of Oregon. These parties are engaged in a kind of undertaking not inherently harmful, but long regarded as useful and meritorious. Certainly there is nothing in the present records to indicate that they have failed to discharge their obligation to patrons, students or the State. And there are no peculiar circumstances or present emergencies which demand extraordinary measures relative to primary education.

Under the doctrine of *Meyer v. Nebraska*, we think it entirely plain that the Act of 1922 unreasonably interferes with the liberty of parents and guardians to direct the upbringing and education of children under their control. As often heretofore pointed out, rights guaranteed by the Constitution may not be abridged by legislation which has no reasonable relation to some purpose within the competency of the State. The fundamental theory of liberty upon which all governments in this Union repose excludes any general power of the State to standardize its children by forcing them to accept instruction from public teachers only. The child is not the mere creature of the State; those who nurture him and direct his destiny have the right, coupled with the high duty, to recognize and prepare him for additional obligations. . . .

Religious Liberty
Cantwell v. Connecticut

No person shall solicit money, services, subscriptions or any valuable thing for any alleged religious, charitable or philanthropic cause . . . unless such cause shall have been approved by the secretary of the public welfare council.
- Connecticut's Religious Solicitation Control Law

On April 26, 1938 Newton Cantwell and his sons, Jesse and Russell, all three ordained ministers of the Jehovah's Witnesses, were arrested on a residential street in New Haven, Connecticut, while soliciting contributions and proselytizing individuals for their religious beliefs.

The Cantwells were charged with multiple violations of Connecticut's religious solicitation control law and with inciting others to breach the peace. Father and sons were tried and convicted in a New Haven County Court of both soliciting religious contributions without prior municipal approval and inciting others to breach the peace by the nature of their solicitation. The three Cantwells appealed for a reversal of their convictions to the Connecticut Supreme Court, asserting that Connecticut's religious solicitation control law was in violation of the Due Process Clause of the Fourteenth Amendment and denied them the First Amendment guarantees of freedom of speech and free exercise of their religion. Connecticut's Supreme Court upheld their religious soliciting convictions. The Cantwells appealed to the United States Supreme Court.

Oral arguments were heard on March 29, 1940 and on May 20, 1940 the 9-0 decision of the Court was announced by Associate Justice Owen Roberts.

THE CANTWELL COURT

Chief Justice Charles Evans Hughes
Appointed Chief Justice by President Hoover
Served 1930 - 1941

Associate Justice James McReynolds
Appointed by President Wilson
Served 1914 - 1941

Associate Justice Pierce Butler
Appointed by President Harding
Served 1922 - 1939

Associate Justice Harlan Fiske Stone
Appointed by President Coolidge
Served 1925 - 1946

Associate Justice Owen Roberts
Appointed by President Hoover
Served 1930 - 1945

Associate Justice Hugo Black
Appointed by President Franklin Roosevelt
Served 1937 - 1971

Associate Justice Stanley Reed
Appointed by President Franklin Roosevelt
Served 1938 - 1957

Associate Justice Felix Frankfurter
Appointed by President Franklin Roosevelt
Served 1939 - 1962

Associate Justice William O. Douglas
Appointed by President Franklin Roosevelt
Served 1939 - 1975

The unedited text of *Cantwell v. Connecticut* can be found on page 296, volume 310 of *United States Reports.*

CANTWELL v. CONNECTICUT
May 20, 1940

JUSTICE ROBERTS: Newton Cantwell and his two sons, Jesse and Russell, members of a group known as Jehovah's Witnesses, and claiming to be ordained ministers, were arrested in New Haven, Connecticut, and each was charged . . . in five counts, with statutory and common law offenses. After trial in the Court of Common Pleas of New Haven County each of them was convicted on the third count, which charged a violation of Section 6294 of the General Statutes of Connecticut, and on the fifth count, which charged commission of the common law offense of inciting a breach of the peace. On appeal to the [Connecticut] Supreme Court the conviction of all three on the third count was affirmed [upheld]. The conviction of Jesse Cantwell, on the fifth count, was also affirmed, but the conviction of Newton and Russell on that count was reversed and a new trial ordered as to them.

. . . [T]he appellants [the Cantwells] pressed the contention that the statute under which the third count was drawn was offensive to the due process clause of the Fourteenth Amendment because . . . it denied them freedom of speech and prohibited their free exercise of religion. In like manner they made the point that they could not be found guilty on the fifth count, without violation of the Amendment.

We have jurisdiction [authority] on appeal from the judgments on the third count. . . . Since the conviction on the fifth count was not based upon a statute, but presents a substantial question under the federal Constitution, we granted the writ of certiorari [agreed to hear the case] in respect of it.

The facts adduced [given] to sustain [uphold] the convictions on the third count follow. On the day of their arrest the [Cantwells] were engaged in going singly from house to house on Cassius Street in New Haven. They were individually equipped with a bag containing books and pamphlets on religious subjects, a portable phonograph and a set of records, each of which, when played, introduced, and was a description of, one of the books. Each [Cantwell] asked the person who responded to his call for permission to play one of the records. If permission was granted he asked the person to buy the book described and, upon refusal, he solicited such contribution towards the publication of the pamphlets as the listener was willing to make. If a contribution was received a pamphlet was delivered upon condition that it would be read.

Cassius Street is in a thickly populated neighborhood, where about ninety per cent of the residents are Roman Catholics. A phonograph record, describing a book entitled "Enemies," included an attack on the Catholic religion. None of the persons interviewed were members of Jehovah's Witnesses.

The statute under which the [Cantwells] were charged provides:

"No person shall solicit money, services, subscriptions or any valuable thing for any alleged religious, charitable or philanthropic cause, from other than a member of the organization for whose benefit such person is soliciting or within the county in which such person or organization is located unless such cause shall have been approved by the secretary of the public welfare council. Upon application of any person in behalf of such cause, the secretary shall determine whether such cause is a religious one or is a bona fide object of charity or philanthropy and conforms to reasonable standards of efficiency and integrity, and, if he shall so find, shall approve the same and issue to the authority in charge a certificate to that effect. Such certificate may be revoked at any time. Any person violating any provision of this section shall be fined not more than one hundred dollars or imprisoned not more than thirty days or both."

The [Cantwells] claimed that their activities were not within the statute but consisted only of distribution of books, pamphlets, and periodicals. The State Supreme Court construed [interpreted] the finding of the trial court to be that "in addition to the sale of the books and the distribution of the pamphlets the defendants [Cantwells] were also soliciting contributions or donations of money for an alleged religious cause, and thereby came within the purview of the statute." It overruled the contention that the Act, as applied to the [Cantwells], offends the due process clause of the Fourteenth Amendment, because it abridges or denies religious freedom and liberty of speech and press. The court stated that it was the solicitation that brought the [Cantwells] within the sweep of the Act and not their other activities in the dissemination of literature. It declared the legislation constitutional as an effort by the State to protect the public against fraud and imposition in the solicitation of funds for what purported to be religious, charitable, or philanthropic causes.

The facts which were held to support the conviction of Jesse Cantwell on the fifth count were that he stopped two men in the street, asked, and received, permission to play a phonograph record, and played the record "Enemies," which attacked the religion and church of the two men, who were Catholics. Both were incensed by the contents of the record and were tempted to strike Cantwell unless he went away. On being told to be on his way he left their presence. There was no evidence that he was personally offensive or entered into any argument with those he interviewed.

The court held that the charge was not assault or breach of the peace or threats on Cantwell's part, but invoking or inciting others to breach of the peace, and that the facts supported the conviction of that offense.

First. We hold that the statute, as construed and applied to the [Cantwells], deprives them of their liberty without due process of law in contravention [violation] of the Fourteenth Amendment. The fundamental concept of liberty embodied in that Amendment embraces the liberties guaranteed by the First Amendment. The First Amendment declares that Congress shall make no law respecting an establishment of religion or prohibiting the free exercise thereof. The Fourteenth Amendment has rendered the legislatures of the states as incompetent as Congress to enact such laws. The constitutional inhibition of legislation on the subject of religion has a double aspect. On the one hand, it forestalls compulsion by law of the acceptance of any creed or the practice of any form of worship. Freedom of conscience and freedom to adhere to such religious organization or form of worship as the individual may choose cannot be restricted by law. On the other hand, it safeguards the free exercise of the chosen form of religion. Thus the Amendment embraces two concepts - freedom to believe and freedom to act. The first is absolute but, in the nature of things, the second cannot be.

Conduct remains subject to regulation for the protection of society. The freedom to act must have appropriate definition to preserve the enforcement of that protection. In every case the power to regulate must be so exercised as not, in attaining a permissible end, unduly to infringe the protected freedom. No one would contest the proposition that a state may not, by statute, wholly deny the right to preach or to disseminate religious views. Plainly such a previous and absolute restraint would violate the terms of the guaranty. It is equally clear that a state may by general and nondiscriminatory legislation regulate the times, the places, and the manner of soliciting upon its streets, and of holding meetings thereon; and may in other respects safeguard the peace, good order and comfort of the community, without unconstitutionally invading the liberties protected by the Fourteenth Amendment. The [Cantwells] are right in their insistence that the Act in question is not such a regulation. If a certificate is procured, solicitation is permitted without restraint but, in the absence of a certificate, solicitation is altogether prohibited.

The [Cantwells] urge that to require them to obtain a certificate as a condition of soliciting support for their views amounts to a prior restraint on the exercise of their religion within the meaning of the Constitution. The State insists that the Act, as construed by the Supreme Court of Connecticut, imposes no previous restraint upon the dissemination of religious views or teaching but merely safeguards against the perpetration of frauds under the cloak of religion. Conceding that this is so, the question remains whether the method adopted by Connecticut to that end transgresses the liberty safeguarded by the Constitution.

The general regulation, in the public interest, of solicitation, which does not involve any religious test and does not unreasonably obstruct or delay the collection of funds, is not open to any constitutional objection, even though the collection be for a religious purpose. Such regulation would not constitute a prohibited previous restraint on the free exercise of religion or interpose an inadmissible obstacle to its exercise.

It will be noted, however, that the Act requires an application to the secretary of the public welfare council of the State; that he is empowered to determine whether the cause is a religious one, and that the issue of a certificate depends upon his affirmative action. If he finds that the cause is not that of religion, to solicit for it becomes a crime. He is not to issue a certificate as a matter of course. His decision to issue or refuse it involves appraisal of facts, the exercise of judgment, and the formation of an opinion. He is authorized to withhold his approval if he determines that the cause is not a religious one. Such a censorship of religion as the means of determining its right to survive is a denial of liberty protected by the First Amendment and included in the liberty which is within the protection of the Fourteenth.

The State asserts that if the licensing officer acts arbitrarily, capriciously, or corruptly, his action is subject to judicial correction. Counsel refer to the rule prevailing in Connecticut that the decision of a commission or an administrative official will be reviewed upon a claim that "it works material damage to individual or corporate rights, or invades or threatens such rights, or is so unreasonable as to justify judicial intervention, or is not consonant with justice, or that a legal duty has not been performed." It is suggested that the statute is to be read as requiring the officer to issue a certificate unless the cause in question is clearly not a religious one; and that if he violates his duty his action will be corrected by a court.

To this suggestion there are several sufficient answers. The line between a discretionary and a ministerial act is not always easy to mark and the statute has not been construed by the State court to impose a mere ministerial duty on the secretary of the welfare council. Upon his decision as to the nature of the cause, the right to solicit depends. Moreover, the availability of a judicial remedy for abuses in the system of licensing still leaves that system one of previous restraint which, in the field of free speech and press, we have held inadmissible. A statute authorizing previous restraint upon the exercise of the guaranteed freedom by judicial decision after trial is as obnoxious to the Constitution as one providing for like restraint by administrative action.

Nothing we have said is intended even remotely to imply that, under the cloak of religion, persons may, with impunity, commit frauds upon the public. Certainly penal laws are available to punish such conduct. Even the exercise of religion may be at some slight inconvenience in order that the state may protect its citizens from injury. Without doubt a state may protect its citizens from fraudulent solicitation by requiring a stranger in the community, before permitting him publicly to solicit funds for any purpose, to establish his identity and his authority to act for the cause which he purports to represent. The state is likewise free to regulate the time and manner of solicitation generally, in the interest of public safety, peace, comfort or convenience. But to condition the solicitation of aid for the perpetuation of religious views or systems upon a license, the grant of which rests in the exercise of a determination by state authority as to what is a religious cause, is to lay a forbidden burden upon the exercise of liberty protected by the Constitution.

Second. We hold that, in the circumstances disclosed, the conviction of Jesse Cantwell on the fifth count must be set aside. Decision as to the lawfulness of the conviction demands the weighing of two conflicting interests. The fundamental law declares the interest of the United States that the free exercise of religion be not prohibited and that freedom to communicate information and opinion be not abridged. The state of Connecticut has an obvious interest in the preservation and protection of peace and good order within her borders. We must determine whether the alleged protection of the State's interest, means to which end would, in the absence of limitation by the federal Constitution, lie wholly within the State's discretion, has been pressed, in this instance, to a point where it has come into fatal collision with the overriding interest protected by the federal compact.

Conviction on the fifth count was not pursuant to a statute evincing a legislative judgment that street discussion of religious affairs, because of its tendency to provoke disorder, should be regulated, or a judgment that the playing of a phonograph on the streets should in the interest of comfort or privacy be limited or prevented. Violation of an Act exhibiting such a legislative judgment and narrowly drawn to prevent the supposed evil, would pose a question differing from that we must here answer. Such a declaration of the State's policy would weigh heavily in any challenge of the law as infringing constitutional limitations. Here, however, the judgment is based on a common law [law based on judicial decisions] concept of the most general and undefined nature. The [lower court] has held that [Cantwell's] conduct constituted the commission of an offense under the State law, and we accept its decision as binding upon us to that extent.

The offense known as breach of the peace embraces a great variety of conduct destroying or menacing public order and tranquillity. It includes not only violent acts but acts and words likely to produce violence in others. No one would have the hardihood to suggest that the principle of freedom of speech sanctions incitement to riot or that religious liberty connotes the privilege to exhort others to physical attack upon those belonging to another sect. When clear and present danger of riot, disorder, interference with traffic upon the public streets, or other immediate threat to public safety, peace, or order, appears, the power of the state to prevent or punish is obvious. Equally obvious is it that a state may not unduly suppress free communication of views, religious or other, under the guise of conserving desirable conditions. Here we have a situation analogous to a conviction under a statute sweeping in a great variety of conduct under a general and indefinite characterization, and leaving to the executive and judicial branches too wide a discretion in its application.

Having these considerations in mind, we note that Jesse Cantwell, on April 26, 1938, was upon a public street, where he had a right to be, and where he had a right peacefully to impart his views to others. There is no showing that his deportment was noisy, truculent, overbearing or offensive. He requested of two pedestrians permission to play to them a phonograph record. The permission was granted. It is not claimed that he intended to insult or affront the hearers by playing the record. It is plain that he wished only to interest them in his propaganda. The sound of the phonograph is not shown to have disturbed residents of the street, to have drawn a crowd, or to have impeded traffic. Thus far he had invaded no right or interest of the public or of the men accosted.

The record played by Cantwell embodies a general attack on all organized religious systems as instruments of Satan and injurious to man; it then singles out the Roman Catholic Church for strictures couched in terms which naturally would offend not only persons of that persuasion, but all others who respect the honestly held religious faith of their fellows. The hearers were in fact highly offended. One of them said he felt like hitting Cantwell and the other that he was tempted to throw Cantwell off the street. The one who testified he felt like hitting Cantwell said, in answer to the question "Did you do anything else or have any other reaction?" "No, sir, because he said he would take the victrola and he went." The other witness testified that he told Cantwell he had better get off the street before something happened to him and that was the end of the matter as Cantwell picked up his books and walked up the street.

Cantwell's conduct, in the view of the [lower court], considered apart from the effect of his communication upon his hearers, did not amount to a breach of the peace. One may, however, be guilty of the offense if he commit acts or make statements likely to provoke violence and disturbance of good order, even though no such eventuality be intended. Decisions to this effect are many, but examination discloses that, in practically all, the provocative language which was held to amount to a breach of the peace consisted of profane, indecent, or abusive remarks directed to the person of the hearer. Resort to epithets or personal abuse is not in any proper sense communication of information or opinion safeguarded by the Constitution, and its punishment as a criminal act would raise no question under that instrument.

We find in [this] case no assault or threatening of bodily harm, no truculent bearing, no intentional discourtesy, no personal abuse. On the contrary, we find only an effort to persuade a willing listener to buy a book or to contribute money in the interest of what Cantwell, however misguided others may think him, conceived to be true religion.

In the realm of religious faith, and in that of political belief, sharp differences arise. In both fields the tenets of one man may seem the rankest error to his neighbor. To persuade others to his own point of view, the pleader, as we know, at times, resorts to exaggeration, to vilification of men who have been, or are, prominent in church or state, and even to false statement. But the people of this nation have ordained in the light of history, that, in spite of the probability of excesses and abuses, these liberties are, in the long view, essential to enlightened opinion and right conduct on the part of the citizens of a democracy.

The essential characteristic of these liberties is, that under their shield many types of life, character, opinion and belief can develop unmolested and unobstructed. Nowhere is this shield more necessary than in our own country for a people composed of many races and of many creeds. There are limits to the exercise of these liberties. The danger in these times from the coercive activities of those who in the delusion of racial or religious conceit would incite violence and breaches of the peace in order to deprive others of their equal right to the exercise of their liberties, is emphasized by events familiar to all. These and other transgressions of those limits the states appropriately may punish.

Although the contents of the record not unnaturally aroused animosity, we think that, in the absence of a statute narrowly drawn to define and punish specific conduct as constituting a clear and present danger to a substantial interest of the State, [Cantwell]'s communication, considered in the light of the constitutional guaranties, raised no such clear and present menace to public peace and order as to render him liable to conviction of the common law offense in question.

The judgment affirming the convictions on the third and fifth counts is reversed and the cause is remanded [returned to the lower court] for further proceedings not inconsistent with this opinion.

Reversed.

Public Money For Religious Purposes
Everson v. Ewing Board of Education

Whenever in any district there are children living remote from any schoolhouse the Board of Education may make contracts for the transportation of such children to and from school, including the transportation of school children to and from any school other than a public school.

- **New Jersey's Student Transportation Law**

Pursuant to New Jersey's Student Transportation Law the School Board of the Township of Ewing, New Jersey, passed a reimbursement resolution authorizing the repayment, from public tax money, of transit fares paid by parents for their children's fare to and from the community's public *and parochial* schools.

Arch Everson, a taxpayer living in the school district, sued the Ewing School Board in a New Jersey Court, asserting that their authorizing the use of public tax money for the transportation of students to and from a parochial school violated the First Amendment's Establishment Clause. Everson asked that both the School Board's Reimbursement Resolution and New Jersey's Student Transportation Law, on which it was based, be held unconstitutional. The trial court found that the New Jersey State Legislature had wrongly enacted the Student Transportation Law and struck it and the School Board's Reimbursement Resolution down. The School Board appealed to the New Jersey Court of Errors and Appeals, which reversed the lower Court, finding that the Resolution and the Law were not in conflict with the Constitution's First Amendment. Everson appealed to the United States Supreme Court.

Oral arguments were heard on November 20, 1946 and the 5-4 decision of the Court was announced on February 10, 1947 by Associate Justice Hugo Black.

THE EVERSON COURT

Chief Justice Fred Vinson
Appointed Chief Justice by President Truman
Served 1946 - 1953

Associate Justice Hugo Black
Appointed by President Franklin Roosevelt
Served 1937 - 1971

Associate Justice Stanley Reed
Appointed by President Franklin Roosevelt
Served 1938 - 1957

Associate Justice Felix Frankfurter
Appointed by President Franklin Roosevelt
Served 1939 - 1962

Associate Justice William O. Douglas
Appointed by President Franklin Roosevelt
Served 1939 - 1975

Associate Justice Frank Murphy
Appointed by President Franklin Roosevelt
Served 1940 - 1949

Associate Justice Robert Jackson
Appointed by President Franklin Roosevelt
Served 1941 - 1954

Associate Justice Wiley Rutledge
Appointed by President Franklin Roosevelt
Served 1943 - 1949

Associate Justice Harold Burton
Appointed by President Truman
Served 1945 - 1958

The unedited text of *Everson v. Ewing Board of Education* can be found on page 1, volume 330 of *United States Reports.*

EVERSON v. EWING TOWNSHIP
BOARD OF EDUCATION
February 10, 1947

JUSTICE BLACK: A New Jersey statute authorizes its local school districts to make rules and contracts for the transportation of children to and from schools. The appellee, [Ewing] township board of education, acting pursuant to this statute, authorized reimbursement to parents of money expended by them for the bus transportation of their children on regular busses operated by the public transportation system. Part of this money was for the payment of transportation of some children in the community to Catholic parochial schools. These church schools give their students, in addition to secular education, regular religious instruction conforming to the religious tenets and modes of worship of the Catholic Faith. The superintendent of these schools is a Catholic priest.

The appellant [Everson], in his capacity as a district taxpayer, filed suit in a state court challenging the right of the Board to reimburse parents of parochial school students. He contended that the statute and the resolution passed pursuant to it violated both the State and the Federal Constitutions. That court held that the legislature was without power to authorize such payment under the state constitution. The New Jersey Court of Errors and Appeals reversed, holding that neither the statute nor the resolution passed pursuant to it was in conflict with the State constitution or the provisions of the Federal Constitution in issue. The case is here on appeal. . . .

The only contention here is that the state statute and the resolution, insofar as they authorized reimbursement to parents of children attending parochial schools, violate the Federal Constitution. . . . The statute and the resolution forced inhabitants to pay taxes to help support and maintain schools which are dedicated to, and which regularly teach, the Catholic Faith. This is alleged to be a use of state power to support church schools contrary to the prohibition of the First Amendment which the Fourteenth Amendment made applicable to the states.

. . . . The New Jersey statute is challenged as a "law respecting an establishment of religion." The First Amendment, as made applicable to the states by the Fourteenth, commands that a state "shall make no law respecting an establishment of religion, or prohibiting the free exercise thereof. . . ." These words of the First Amendment reflected in the minds of early Americans a vivid mental picture of conditions and practices which they fervently wished to stamp out in order to preserve liberty for themselves and for their posterity. Doubtless their goal has not been entirely reached; but so far has the Nation moved toward it that the expression "law respecting an establishment of religion," probably does not so vividly remind present-day Americans of the evils, fears, and political problems that caused that expression to be written into our Bill of Rights. Whether this New Jersey law is one respecting an "establishment of religion" requires an understanding of the meaning of that language, particularly with respect to the imposition of taxes. Once again, therefore, it is not inappropriate briefly to review the background and environment of the period in which that constitutional language was fashioned and adopted.

A large proportion of the early settlers of this country came here from Europe to escape the bondage of laws which compelled them to support and attend government-favored churches. The centuries immediately before and contemporaneous with the colonization of America had been filled with turmoil, civil strife, and persecutions, generated in large part by established sects determined to maintain their absolute political and religious supremacy. With the power of government supporting them, at various times and places, Catholics had persecuted Protestants, Protestants had persecuted Catholics, Protestant sects had persecuted other Protestant sects, Catholics of one shade of belief had persecuted Catholics of another shade of belief, and all of these had from time to time persecuted Jews. In efforts to force loyalty to whatever religious group happened to be on top and in league with the government of a particular time and place, men and women had been fined, cast in jail, cruelly tortured, and killed. Among the offenses for which these punishments had been inflicted were such things as speaking disrespectfully of the views of ministers of government-established churches, non-attendance at those churches, expressions of non-belief in their doctrines, and failure to pay taxes and tithes to support them.

These practices of the old world were transplanted and began to thrive in the soil of the new America. The very charters granted by the English Crown to the individuals and companies designated to make the laws which would control the destinies of the colonials authorized these individuals and companies to erect religious establishments which all, whether believers or non-believers, would be required to support and attend. An exercise of this authority was accompanied by a repetition of many of the old-world practices and persecutions. Catholics found themselves hounded and proscribed because of their faith; Quakers who followed their conscience went to jail; Baptists were peculiarly obnoxious to certain dominant Protestant sects; men and women of varied faiths who happened to be in a minority in a particular locality were persecuted because they steadfastly persisted in worshipping God only as their own consciences dictated. And all of these dissenters were compelled to pay tithes and taxes to support government-sponsored churches whose ministers preached inflammatory sermons designed to strengthen and consolidate the established faith by generating a burning hatred against dissenters.

These practices became so commonplace as to shock the freedom-loving colonials into a feeling of abhorrence. The imposition of taxes to pay ministers' salaries and to build and maintain churches and church property aroused their indignation. It was these feelings which found expression in the First Amendment. No one locality and no one group throughout the Colonies can rightly be given entire credit for having aroused the sentiment that culminated in adoption of the Bill of Rights' provisions embracing religious liberty. But Virginia, where the established church had achieved a dominant influence in political affairs and where many excesses attracted wide public attention, provided a great stimulus and able leadership for the movement. The people there, as elsewhere, reached the conviction that individual religious liberty could be achieved best under a government which was stripped of all power to tax, to support, or otherwise to assist any or all religions, or to interfere with the beliefs of any religious individual or group.

The movement toward this end reached its dramatic climax in Virginia in 1785-86 when the Virginia legislative body was about to renew Virginia's tax levy for the support of the established church. Thomas Jefferson and James Madison led the fight against this tax. Madison wrote his great Memorial and Remonstrance against the law. In it, he eloquently argued that a true religion did not need the support of law; that no person, either believer or non-believer, should be taxed to support a religious institution of any kind; that the best interest of a society required that the minds of men always be wholly free; and that cruel persecutions were the inevitable result of government-established religions. Madison's Remonstrance received strong support throughout Virginia, and the Assembly postponed consideration of the proposed tax measure until its next session. When the proposal came up for consideration at that session, it not only died in committee, but the Assembly enacted the famous "Virginia Bill for Religious Liberty" originally written by Thomas Jefferson. The preamble to that Bill stated among other things that

"Almighty God hath created the mind free; that all attempts to influence it by temporal punishments or burthens, or by civil incapacitations, tend only to beget habits of hypocrisy and meanness, and are a departure from the plan of the Holy author of our religion, who being Lord both of body and mind, yet chose not to propagate it by coercions on either . . . ; that to compel a man to furnish contributions of money for the propagation of opinions which he disbelieves, is sinful and tyrannical; that even the forcing him to support this or that teacher of his own religious persuasion, is depriving him of the comfortable liberty of giving his contributions to the particular pastor, whose morals he would make his pattern. . . ."

And the statute itself enacted

> "That no man shall be compelled to frequent or
> support any religious worship, place, or ministry
> whatsoever, nor shall be enforced, restrained, mo-
> lested, or burthened in his body or goods, nor
> shall otherwise suffer on account of his religious
> opinions or belief." . . .

This Court has previously recognized that the provisions
of the First Amendment, in the drafting and adoption of
which Madison and Jefferson played such leading roles,
had the same objective and were intended to provide the
same protection against governmental intrusion on religious liberty as the Virginia statute. Prior to the adoption
of the Fourteenth Amendment, the First Amendment did
not apply as a restraint against the states. Most of them
did soon provide similar constitutional protections for
religious liberty. . . .

The meaning and scope of the First Amendment, preventing establishment of religion or prohibiting the free exercise thereof, in the light of its history and the evils it was
designed forever to suppress, have been several times
elaborated by the decisions of this Court prior to the application of the First Amendment to the states by the
Fourteenth. The broad meaning given the Amendment by
these earlier cases has been accepted by this Court in its
decisions concerning an individuals' religious freedom
rendered since the Fourteenth Amendment was interpreted to make the prohibitions of the First applicable to state
action abridging religious freedom. There is every reason
to give the same application and broad interpretation to
the "establishment of religion" clause. The interrelation

of these complementary clauses was well summarized in a statement of the Court of Appeals of South Carolina . . . :

> "The structure of our government has, for the preservation of civil liberty, rescued the temporal institutions from religious interference. On the other hand, it has secured religious liberty from the invasion of the civil authority."

The "establishment of religion" clause of the First Amendment means at least this: Neither a state nor the Federal Government can set up a church. Neither can pass laws which aid one religion, aid all religions, or prefer one religion over another. Neither can force nor influence a person to go to or to remain away from church against his will or force him to profess a belief or disbelief in any religion. No person can be punished for entertaining or professing religious beliefs or disbeliefs, for church attendance or non-attendance. No tax in any amount, large or small, can be levied to support any religious activities or institutions, whatever they may be called, or whatever form they may adopt to teach or practice religion. Neither a state nor the Federal Government can, openly or secretly, participate in the affairs of any religious organizations or groups and *vice versa.* In the words of Jefferson, the clause against establishment of religion by law was intended to erect "a wall of separation between church and State."

. . . . The First Amendment has erected a wall between church and state. That wall must be kept high and impregnable. We could not approve the slightest breach. New Jersey has not breached it here.

Affirmed [upheld].

Early Release Time
For Religious Instruction
Zorach v. Clauson

Absence for religious observance and education shall be permitted under the rules that the Commissioner of Education of the State of New York shall establish.

- New York State's Early Release Law

The Board of Education of the City of New York, in accordance with the rules established by the New York State Commissioner of Education, created an Early Release Time Program in the New York City Public Schools.

Under the Early Release Time Program, New York City public school students were permitted, at the written request of their parents, to leave school up to one hour early one day a week to go to their respective religious institutions for instruction or observance. The Early Release Time Program did not involve either religious instruction or observance in the classroom or the expenditure of public funds for religious instruction or observance.

The Early Release Time Program was challenged by several parents of New York City school students, including Tessim Zorach, who sued the Board of Education of the City of New York and its President, Andrew Clauson, in the New York Courts, contending that the program was a violation of the First Amendment's Religion Clauses.

The New York State Court of Appeals upheld the constitutionality of the Early Release Time Program, finding that the program neither prohibited the "free exercise " of religion nor made a law "respecting an establishment of religion." Zorach appealed to the U.S. Supreme Court.

Oral arguments were heard on January 31 and February 1, 1952. The 6-3 decision of the Court was announced on April 28, 1952 by Associate Justice William O. Douglas.

THE ZORACH COURT

Chief Justice Fred Vinson
Appointed Chief Justice by President Truman
Served 1946 - 1953

Associate Justice Hugo Black
Appointed by President Franklin Roosevelt
Served 1937 -1971

Associate Justice Stanley Reed
Appointed by President Franklin Roosevelt
Served 1938- 1957

Associate Justice Felix Frankfurter
Appointed by President Franklin Roosevelt
Served 1939 - 1962

Associate Justice William O. Douglas
Appointed by President Franklin Roosevelt
Served 1939 - 1975

Associate Justice Robert Jackson
Appointed by President Franklin Roosevelt
Served 1941 - 1954

Associate Justice Harold Burton
Appointed by President Truman
Served 1945 - 1958

Associate Justice Tom Clark
Appointed by President Truman
Served 1949 - 1967

Associate Justice Sherman Minton
Appointed by President Truman
Served 1949 - 1956

The unedited text of *Zorach v. Clauson* can be found on page 306, volume 343 of *United States Reports.*

ZORACH v. CLAUSON
April 28, 1952

JUSTICE DOUGLAS: New York City has a program which permits its public schools to release students during the school day so that they may leave the school buildings and school grounds and go to religious centers for religious instruction or devotional exercises. A student is released on written request of his parents. Those not released stay in the classrooms. The churches make weekly reports to the schools, sending a list of children who have been released from public school but who have not reported for religious instruction.

This "released time" program involves neither religious instruction in public school classrooms nor the expenditure of public funds. All costs, including the application blanks, are paid by the religious organizations. The case is therefore unlike *McCollum v. Board of Education*, which involved a "released time" program from Illinois. In that case the classrooms were turned over to religious instructors. We accordingly held that the program violated the First Amendment which (by reason of the Fourteenth Amendment) prohibits the states from establishing religion or prohibiting its free exercise.

Appellants [Zorach et al.], who are taxpayers and residents of New York City and whose children attend its public schools, challenge the present law, contending it is in essence not different from the one involved in the *McCollum* case. Their argument, stated elaborately in various ways, reduces itself to this: the weight and influence of the school is put behind a program for religious instruction; public school teachers police it, keeping tab on students who are released; the classroom activities come to a halt while the students who are released for religious instruction are on leave; the school is a crutch on which the churches are leaning for support in their religious training; without the cooperation of the schools this "released time" program, like the one in the *McCollum* case, would be futile and ineffective. The New York Court of Appeals sustained [upheld] the law against this claim of unconstitutionality. The case is here on appeal.

. . . . It takes obtuse reasoning to inject any issue of the "free exercise" of religion into the present case. No one is forced to go to the religious classroom and no religious exercise or instruction is brought to the classrooms of the public schools. A student need not take religious instruction. He is left to his own desires as to the manner or time of his religious devotions, if any.

There is a suggestion that the system involves the use of coercion to get public school students into religious classrooms. There is no evidence in the record before us that supports that conclusion. The present record indeed tells us that the school authorities are neutral in this regard and do no more than release students whose parents so request. If in fact coercion were used, if it were established that any one or more teachers were using their office to persuade or force students to take the religious instruction, a wholly different case would be presented. Hence we put aside that claim of coercion both as respects the "free exercise" of religion and "an establishment of religion" within the meaning of the First Amendment.

Moreover, apart from that claim of coercion, we do not see how New York by this type of "released time" program has made a law respecting an establishment of religion within the meaning of the First Amendment. There is much talk of the separation of Church and State in the history of the Bill of Rights and in the decisions clustering around the First Amendment. There cannot be the slightest doubt that the First Amendment reflects the philosophy that Church and State should be separated. And so far as interference with the "free exercise" of religion and an "establishment" of religion are concerned, the separation must be complete and unequivocal. The First Amendment within the scope of its coverage permits no exception; the prohibition is absolute. The First Amendment, however, does not say that in every and all respects there shall be a separation of Church and State. Rather, it studiously defines the manner, the specific ways, in which there shall be no concert or union or dependency one on the other. That is the common sense of the matter. Otherwise, the state and religion would be aliens to each other - hostile, suspicious, and even unfriendly. Churches could not be required to pay even property taxes. Municipalities would not be permitted to render police or fire protection to religious groups. Policemen who helped parishioners into their places of worship would violate the Constitution. Prayers in our legislative halls; the appeals to the Almighty in the messages of the Chief Executive; the proclamations making Thanksgiving Day a holiday; "so help me God" in our courtroom oaths - these and all other references to the Almighty that run through our laws, our public rituals, our ceremonies would be flouting the First Amendment. A fastidious atheist or agnostic could even object to the supplication with which the Court opens each session: "God save the United States and this Honorable Court."

We would have to press the concept of separation of Church and State to these extremes to condemn the present law on constitutional grounds. The nullification of this law would have wide and profound effects. A Catholic student applies to his teacher for permission to leave the school during hours on a Holy Day of Obligation to attend a mass. A Jewish student asks his teacher for permission to be excused for Yom Kippur. A Protestant wants the afternoon off for a family baptismal ceremony. In each case the teacher requires parental consent in writing. In each case the teacher, in order to make sure the student is not a truant, goes further and requires a report from the priest, the rabbi, or the minister. The teacher in other words cooperates in a religious program to the extent of making it possible for her students to participate in it. Whether she does it occasionally for a few students, regularly for one, or pursuant to a systematized program designed to further the religious needs of all the students does not alter the character of the act.

We are a religious people whose institutions presuppose a Supreme Being. We guarantee the freedom to worship as one chooses. We make room for as wide a variety of beliefs and creeds as the spiritual needs of man deem necessary. We sponsor an attitude on the part of government that shows no partiality to any one group and that lets each flourish according to the zeal of its adherents and the appeal of its dogma. When the state encourages religious instruction or cooperates with religious authorities by adjusting the schedule of public events to sectarian needs, it follows the best of our traditions. For it then respects the religious nature of our people and accommodates the public service to their spiritual needs. To hold that it may not would be to find in the Constitution a requirement that the government show a callous indifference to religious groups. That would be preferring those who believe in no religion over those who do believe. Government may not finance religious groups nor undertake religious instruction nor blend secular and sectarian education nor use secular institutions to force one or some religion on any person. But we find no constitutional requirement which makes it necessary for government to be hostile to religion and to throw its weight against efforts to widen the effective scope of religious influence. The government must be neutral when it comes to competition between sects. It may not thrust any sect on any person. It may not make a religious observance compulsory. It may not coerce anyone to attend church, to observe a religious holiday, or to take religious instruction. But it can close its doors or suspend its operations as to those who want to repair to their religious sanctuary for worship or instruction. No more than that is undertaken here.

This program may be unwise and improvident from an educational or a community viewpoint. That appeal is made to us on a theory, previously advanced, that each case must be decided on the basis of "our own prepossessions." Our individual preferences, however, are not the constitutional standard. The constitutional standard is the separation of Church and State. The problem, like many problems in constitutional law, is one of degree.

In the *McCollum* case the classrooms were used for religious instruction and the force of the public school was used to promote that instruction. Here, as we have said, the public schools do no more than accommodate their schedules to a program of outside religious instruction. We follow the *McCollum* case. But we cannot expand it to cover the present released time program unless separation of Church and State means that public institutions can make no adjustments of their schedules to accommodate the religious needs of the people. We cannot read into the Bill of Rights such a philosophy of hostility to religion.

Affirmed [upheld].

School Prayer
Engel v. Vitale

Almighty God, we acknowledge our dependence upon Thee, and we beg Thy blessings upon us, our parents, our teachers, and our Country.

- The New York "Regent's Prayer"

The New York Board of Regents, a governmental agency charged with supervision of New York State's public school system, composed a "non-denominational" official school prayer, which they recommended for daily classroom recitation. Any student not wanting to recite the "Regents Prayer" was permitted to either remain silent or leave the classroom. The Regents, in their *Statement on Moral and Spiritual Training in the Schools*, said: "We believe that this [prayer] will be subscribed to by all men and women of good will, and we call upon all of them to aid in giving life to our program."

The Board of Education of New Hyde Park, a School District located on Long Island, New York, directed, as recommended by the New York State Regents, that its principals require their students to recite the official "Regents Prayer" aloud at the beginning of each school day.

Several New Hyde Park parents, including Stephen Engel, objected to the daily recitation of the "Regents Prayer" in their children's classroom. Alleging that it was as a violation of the First Amendment's Establishment Clause, they brought suit against William Vitale, Jr., President of the School Board. Three New York Courts - the Nassau County Court, the New York Court of Appeals, and the New York Supreme Court - all found for the School District. Engel appealed to the United States Supreme Court.

Oral arguments were heard on April 3, 1962 and the 6-1 decision of the Court was announced on June 25, 1962 by Associate Justice Hugo Black.

THE ENGEL COURT

Chief Justice Earl Warren
Appointed Chief Justice by President Eisenhower
Served 1953 - 1969

Associate Justice Hugo Black
Appointed by President Franklin Roosevelt
Served 1937 - 1971

Associate Justice William O. Douglas
Appointed by President Franklin Roosevelt
Served 1939 - 1975

Associate Justice Tom Clark
Appointed by President Truman
Served 1949 - 1967

Associate Justice John Marshall Harlan
Appointed by President Eisenhower
Served 1955 -1971

Associate Justice William Brennan
Appointed by President Eisenhower
Served 1956 - 1990

Associate Justice Potter Stewart
Appointed by President Eisenhower
Served 1958 - 1981

The unedited text of *Engel v. Vitale* can be found on page 421, volume 370 of *United States Reports.*

ENGEL v. VITALE
June 25, 1962

JUSTICE HUGO BLACK: The respondent Board of Education of Union Free School District No. 9, New Hyde Park, New York, acting in its official capacity under state law, directed the School District's principal to cause the following prayer to be said aloud by each class in the presence of a teacher at the beginning of each school day:

> "Almighty God, we acknowledge our dependence upon Thee, and we beg Thy blessings upon us, our parents, our teachers and our Country."

This daily procedure was adopted on the recommendation of the State Board of Regents, a governmental agency created by the State Constitution to which the New York Legislature has granted broad supervisory, executive, and legislative powers over the State's public school system. These state officials composed the prayer which they recommended and published as a part of their "Statement on Moral and Spiritual Training in the Schools," saying: "We believe that this Statement will be subscribed to by all men and women of good will, and we call upon all of them to aid in giving life to our program."

Shortly after the practice of reciting the Regents' prayer was adopted by the School District, the parents of ten pupils brought this action in a New York State Court insisting that use of this official prayer in the public schools was contrary to the beliefs, religions, or religious practices of both themselves and their children. Among other things, these parents challenged the constitutionality of both the state law authorizing the School District to direct the use of prayer in public schools and the School District's regulation ordering the recitation of this particular prayer on the ground that these actions of official governmental agencies violate that part of the First Amendment of the Federal Constitution which commands that "Congress shall make no law respecting an establishment of religion" - a command which was "made applicable to the State of New York by the Fourteenth Amendment of the said Constitution." The New York Court of Appeals, over the dissents of Judges Dye and Fuld, sustained [let stand] an order of the lower state courts which had upheld the power of New York to use the Regents' prayer as a part of the daily procedures of its public schools so long as the schools did not compel any pupil to join in the prayer over his or his parents' objection. We granted certiorari [agreed to] review this important decision involving rights protected by the First and Fourteenth Amendments.

We think that by using its public school system to encourage recitation of the Regents' prayer, the State of New York has adopted a practice wholly inconsistent with the Establishment Clause. There can, of course, be no doubt that New York's program of daily classroom invocation of God's blessings as prescribed in the Regents' prayer is a religious activity. It is a solemn avowal of divine faith and supplication for the blessings of the Almighty. The nature of such a prayer has always been religious, none of the [members of the School Board] has denied this and the trial court expressly so found:

> "The religious nature of prayer was recognized by Jefferson and has been concurred in by theological writers, the United States Supreme Court and State courts and administrative officials, including New York's Commissioner of Education.

A committee of the New York Legislature has agreed.

"The Board of Regents . . . , the [School Board] and [other interested parties] all concede the religious nature of prayer, but seek to distinguish this prayer because it is based on our spiritual heritage. . . ."

The petitioners contend among other things that the state laws requiring or permitting use of the Regents' prayer must be struck down as a violation of the Establishment Clause [of the First Amendment] because that prayer was composed by governmental officials as a part of a governmental program to further religious beliefs. For this reason, petitioners argue, the State's use of the Regents' prayer in its public school system breaches the constitutional wall of separation between Church and State. We agree with that contention since we think that the constitutional prohibition against laws respecting an establishment of religion must at least mean that in this country it is no part of the business of government to compose official prayers for any group of the American people to recite as a part of a religious program carried on by government.

It is a matter of history that this very practice of establishing governmentally composed prayers for religious services was one of the reasons which caused many of our early colonists to leave England and seek religious freedom in America. The Book of Common Prayer, which was created under governmental direction and which was approved by Acts of Parliament in 1548 and 1549, set out in minute detail the accepted form and content of prayer and other religious ceremonies to be used in the established, tax-supported Church of England. The controversies over the Book and what should be its content repeatedly threatened to disrupt the peace of that country as the accepted forms of prayer in the established church changed with the views of the particular ruler that happened to be in control at the time. Powerful groups representing some of the varying religious views of the people struggled among themselves to impress their particular views upon the Government and obtain amendments of the Book more suitable to their respective notions of how religious services should be conducted in order that the official religious establishment would advance their particular religious beliefs. Other groups, lacking the necessary political power to influence the Government on the matter, decided to leave England and its established church and seek freedom in America from England's governmentally ordained and supported religion.

It is an unfortunate fact of history that when some of the very groups which had most strenuously opposed the established Church of England found themselves sufficiently in control of colonial governments in this country to write their own prayers into law, they passed laws making their own religion the official religion of their respective colonies. Indeed, as late as the time of the Revolutionary War, there were established churches in at least eight of the thirteen former colonies and established religions in at least four of the other five. But the successful Revolution against English political domination was shortly followed by intense opposition to the practice of establishing religion by law. This opposition crystallized rapidly into an effective political force in Virginia where the minority religious groups such as Presbyterians, Lutherans, Quakers and Baptists had gained such strength that the adherents to the established Episcopal Church were actually a minority themselves. In 1785-1786, those opposed to the established Church, led by James Madison and Thomas Jefferson, who, though themselves not members of any of these dissenting religious groups, opposed all religious establishments by law on grounds of principle, obtained the enactment of the famous "Virginia Bill for Religious Liberty" by which all religious groups were placed on an equal footing so far as the State was concerned. Similar though less far-reaching legislation was being considered and passed in other States.

By the time of the adoption of the Constitution, our history shows that there was a widespread awareness among many Americans of the dangers of a union of Church and State. These people knew, some of them from bitter personal experience, that one of the greatest dangers to the freedom of the individual to worship in his own way lay in the Government's placing its official stamp of approval upon one particular kind of prayer or one particular form of religious services. They knew the anguish, hardship and bitter strife that could come when zealous religious groups struggled with one another to obtain the Government's stamp of approval from each King, Queen, or Protector that came to temporary power. The Constitution was intended to avert a part of this danger by leaving the government of this country in the hands of the people rather than in the hands of any monarch. But this safeguard was not enough. Our Founders were no more willing to let the content of their prayers and their privilege of praying whenever they pleased be influenced by the ballot box than they were to let these vital matters of personal conscience depend upon the succession of monarchs. The First Amendment was added to the Constitution to stand as a guarantee that neither the power nor the prestige of the Federal Government would be used to control, support or influence the kinds of prayer the American people can say - that the people's religions must not be subjected to the pressures of government for change each time a new political administration is elected to office. Under that Amendment's prohibition against governmental establishment of religion, as reinforced by the provisions of the Fourteenth Amendment, government in this country, be it state or federal, is without power to prescribe by law any particular form of prayer which is to be used as an official prayer in carrying on any program of governmentally sponsored religious activity.

There can be no doubt that New York's state prayer program officially establishes the religious beliefs embodied in the Regents' prayer. The [Board's] argument to the contrary, which is largely based upon the contention that the Regents' prayer is "non-denominational" and the fact that the program, as modified and approved by state courts, does not require all pupils to recite the prayer but permits those who wish to do so to remain silent or be excused from the room, ignores the essential nature of the program's constitutional defects. Neither the fact that the prayer may be denominationally neutral nor the fact that its observance on the part of the students is voluntary can serve to free it from the limitations of the Establishment Clause, as it might from the Free Exercise Clause, of the First Amendment, both of which are operative against the States by virtue of the Fourteenth Amendment. Although these two clauses may in certain instances overlap, they forbid two quite different kinds of governmental encroachment upon religious freedom. The Establishment Clause, unlike the Free Exercise Clause, does not depend upon any showing of direct governmental compulsion and is violated by the enactment of laws which establish an official religion whether those laws operate directly to coerce nonobserving individuals or not. This is not to say, of course, that laws officially prescribing a particular form of religious worship do not involve coercion of such individuals. When the power, prestige and financial support of government is placed behind a particular religious belief, the indirect coercive pressure upon religious minorities to conform to the prevailing officially approved religion is plain. But the purposes underlying the Establishment Clause go much further than that. Its first and most immediate purpose rested on the belief that a union of government and religion tends to destroy government and to degrade religion. The history of governmentally established religion, both in England and in this country, showed that whenever government had allied itself with one particular form of religion, the inevitable result had been that it had incurred the hatred, disrespect and even contempt of those who held contrary beliefs. That same history showed that many people had lost their respect for any religion that had relied upon the support of government to spread its faith. The Establishment Clause thus stands as an expression of principle on the part of the Founders of our Constitution that religion is too personal, too sacred, too holy, to permit its "unhallowed perversion" by a civil magistrate. Another purpose of the Establishment Clause rested upon an awareness of the historical fact that governmentally established religions and religious persecutions go hand in hand. The Founders knew that only a few years after the Book of Common Prayer became the only accepted form of religious services in the established Church of England, an Act of Uniformity was passed to compel all Englishmen to attend those services and to make it a criminal offense to conduct or attend religious gatherings of any other kind - a law which was consistently flouted by dissenting religious groups in England and which contributed to widespread persecutions of people like John Bunyan who persisted in holding "unlawful [religious] meetings ... to the great disturbance and distraction of the good subjects of this kingdom. ..." And they knew that similar persecutions had received the sanction of law in several of the colonies in this country soon after the establishment of official religions in those colonies. It was in large part to get completely away from this sort of systematic religious persecution that the Founders brought into being our Nation, our Constitution, and our Bill of Rights with its prohibition against any governmental establishment of religion. The New York laws officially prescribing the Regents' prayer are inconsistent both with the purposes of the Establishment Clause and with the Establishment Clause itself.

It has been argued that to apply the Constitution in such a way as to prohibit state laws respecting an establishment of religious services in public schools is to indicate a hostility toward religion or toward prayer. Nothing, of course, could be more wrong. The history of man is inseparable from the history of religion. And perhaps it is not too much to say that since the beginning of that history many people have devoutly believed that "More things are wrought by prayer than this world dreams of." It was doubtless largely due to men who believed this that there grew up a sentiment that caused men to leave the crosscurrents of officially established state religions and religious persecution in Europe and come to this country filled with the hope that they could find a place in which they could pray when they pleased to the God of their faith in the language they chose. And there were men of this same faith in the power of prayer who led the fight for adoption of our Constitution and also for our Bill of Rights with the very guarantees of religious freedom that forbid the sort of governmental activity which New York has attempted here. These men knew that the First Amendment, which tried to put an end to governmental control of religion and of prayer, was not written to destroy either. They knew rather that it was written to quiet well-justified fears which nearly all of them felt arising out of an awareness that governments of the past had shackled men's tongues to make them speak only the religious thoughts that government wanted them to speak and to pray only to the God that government wanted them to pray to. It is neither sacreligious nor antireligious to say that each separate government in this country should stay out of the business of writing or sanctioning official prayers and leave that purely religious function to the people themselves and to those the people choose to look to for religious guidance.

It is true that New York's establishment of its Regents' prayer as an officially approved religious doctrine of that State does not amount to a total establishment of one particular religious sect to the exclusion of all others - that, indeed, the governmental endorsement of that prayer seems relatively insignificant when compared to the governmental encroachments upon religion which were commonplace two hundred years ago. To those who may subscribe to the view that because the Regents' official prayer is so brief and general there can be no danger to religious freedom in its governmental establishment, however, it may be appropriate to say in the words of James Madison, the author of the First Amendment:

> "[I]t is proper to take alarm at the first experiment on our liberties. . . . Who does not see that the same authority which can establish Christianity, in exclusion of all other Religions, may establish with the same ease any particular sect of

Christians, in exclusion of all other Sects? That the same authority which can force a citizen to contribute three pence only of his property for the support of any one establishment, may force him to conform to any other establishment in all cases whatsoever?"

The judgment of the Court of Appeals of New York is reversed and the cause remanded [sent back to the appropriate lower court for reruling].

Bible Reading In The Public Schools
Abington Schools v. Schempp
Murray v. Curlett

In the beginning God created the heaven and the earth.
- **Genesis, Chapter 1, Verse 1**

The Commonwealth of Pennsylvania required by law that each school day begin with: "At least ten verses from the Holy Bible read, without comment." Students not wishing to participate in the classroom reading could be excused upon written request of their parents. Edward and Sidney Schempp of Philadelphia, members of the Unitarian Church, had all three of their children enrolled in the Abington Schools. The Schempps sued the Abington Schools in U.S. District Court, contending that the Compulsory Bible Readings Law was in violation of the First Amendment's Religion Clauses. The U.S. District Court struck down Pennsylvania's Bible Reading Law. The Abington Schools appealed to the U.S. Supreme Court.

The Baltimore School Commission required by rule that each school day begin with: "Reading, without comment, of a chapter of the Holy Bible and/or the use of the Lord's Prayer." Students not wishing to participate in the classroom reading could be excused upon written request of their parents. Baltimore parent Madalyn Murray and her school-age son, William Murray, atheists, sued the Baltimore School Board in State Court, contending that the Baltimore Schools' Compulsory Bible Readings Rule was a violation of the First Amendment's Religion Clauses. The Maryland Court of Appeals upheld Baltimore's Bible Reading Law. The Murrays appealed to the U.S. Supreme Court.

Oral arguments were heard for the two cases on February 27-28, 1963. The 8-1 decision of the Court was announced on June 17, 1963 by Justice Tom Clark.

THE ABINGTON/MURRAY COURT

Chief Justice Earl Warren
Appointed Chief Justice by President Eisenhower
Served 1953 - 1969

Associate Justice Hugo Black
Appointed by President Franklin Roosevelt
Served 1937 - 1971

Associate Justice William O. Douglas
Appointed by President Franklin Roosevelt
Served 1939 - 1975

Associate Justice Tom Clark
Appointed by President Truman
Served 1949 - 1967

Associate Justice John Marshall Harlan
Appointed by President Eisenhower
Served 1955 -1971

Associate Justice William Brennan
Appointed by President Eisenhower
Served 1956 -1990

Associate Justice Potter Stewart
Appointed by President Eisenhower
Served 1958 - 1981

Associate Justice Byron White
Appointed by President Kennedy
Served 1962 - 1993

Associate Justice Arthur Goldberg
Appointed by President Kennedy
Served 1962 - 1965

The unedited text of *Abington Schools v. Schempp* and *Murray v. Curlett* can be found on page 203, volume 374 of *United States Reports.*

ABINGTON SCHOOLS V. SCHEMPP
MURRAY v. CURLETT
June 17, 1963

JUSTICE CLARK: Once again we are called upon to consider the scope of the provision of the First Amendment to the United States Constitution which declares that "Congress shall make no law respecting an establishment of religion, or prohibiting the free exercise thereof. . . ." These . . . cases present the issues in the context of state action requiring that schools begin each day with readings from the Bible. . . . In light of the history of the First Amendment and of our [previous decisions] interpreting and applying its requirements, we hold that the practices at issue and the laws requiring them are unconstitutional under the Establishment Clause, as applied to the States through the Fourteenth Amendment.

The Commonwealth of Pennsylvania by law requires that "At least ten verses from the Holy Bible shall be read, without comment, at the opening of each public school on each school day. Any child shall be excused from such Bible reading, or attending such Bible reading, upon the written request of his parent or guardian." The Schempp family, husband and wife and two of their three children, brought suit to enjoin [stop] enforcement of the statute, contending that their rights under the Fourteenth Amendment to the Constitution of the United States are, have been, and will continue to be violated unless this statute be declared unconstitutional as violative of these provisions of the First Amendment. . . .

In 1905 the Board of School Commissioners of Baltimore City adopted a rule pursuant to [the] Code of Maryland. The rule provided for the holding of opening exercises in the schools of the city, consisting primarily of the "reading, without comment, of a chapter in the Holy Bible and/or the use of the Lord's Prayer." The petitioners, Mrs. Madalyn Murray and her son, William J. Murray III, are both professed atheists. Following unsuccessful attempts to have the respondent school board rescind the rule, this suit was filed . . . to compel its rescission and cancellation. . . .

It is true that religion has been closely identified with our history and government. As we said in *Engel v. Vitale,* "The history of man is inseparable from the history of religion. And . . . since the beginning of that history many people have devoutly believed that 'More things are wrought by prayer than this world dreams of.'" In *Zorach v. Clauson,* we gave specific recognition to the proposition that "[w]e are a religious people whose institutions presuppose a Supreme Being." The fact that the Founding Fathers believed devotedly that there was a God and that the unalienable rights of man were rooted in Him is clearly evidenced in their writings, from the Mayflower Compact to the Constitution itself. . . .

This is not to say, however, that religion has been so identified with our history and government that religious freedom is not likewise as strongly imbedded in our public and private life. Nothing but the most telling of personal experiences in religious persecution suffered by our forebears could have planted our belief in liberty of religious opinion any more deeply in our heritage. . . . [F]reedom to worship was indispensable in a country whose people came from the four quarters of the earth and brought with them a diversity of religious opinion. . . .

The interrelationship of the Establishment and the Free Exercise Clauses was first touched upon by Justice Roberts for the Court in *Cantwell v. Connecticut*, where it was said that their "inhibition of legislation" had

> "a double aspect. On the one hand, it forestalls compulsion by law of the acceptance of any creed or the practice of any form of worship. Freedom of conscience and freedom to adhere to such religious organization or form of worship as the individual may choose cannot be restricted by law. On the other hand, it safeguards the free exercise of the chosen form of religion. Thus the Amendment embraces two concepts - freedom to believe and freedom to act. The first is absolute but, in the nature of things, the second cannot be."

A half dozen years later in *Everson v. Board of Education*, this Court, through Justice Black, stated that the "scope of the First Amendment . . . was designed forever to suppress" the establishment of religion or the prohibition of the free exercise thereof. In short, the Court held that the Amendment

> "requires the state to be a neutral in its relations with groups of religious believers and non-believers; it does not require the state to be their adversary. State power is no more to be used so as to handicap religions than it is to favor them."

. . . . In 1952 in *Zorach v. Clauson*, Justice Douglas for the Court reiterated:

"There cannot be the slightest doubt that the First Amendment reflects the philosophy that Church and State should be separated. And so far as interference with the 'free exercise' of religion and an 'establishment' of religion are concerned, the separation must be complete and unequivocal. The First Amendment within the scope of its coverage permits no exception; the prohibition is absolute. The First Amendment, however, does not say that in every and all respects there shall be a separation of Church and State. Rather, it studiously defines the manner, the specific ways, in which there shall be no concert or union or dependency one on the other. That is the common sense of the matter."

. . . . In discussing the reach of the Establishment and Free Exercise Clauses of the First Amendment the Court said:

"Although these two clauses may in certain instances overlap, they forbid two quite different kinds of governmental encroachment upon religious freedom. The Establishment Clause, unlike the Free Exercise Clause, does not depend upon any showing of direct governmental compulsion and is violated by the enactment of laws which establish an official religion whether those laws operate directly to coerce non-observing individuals or not. This is not to say, of course, that laws officially prescribing a particular form of religious worship do not involve coercion of such individuals. When the power, prestige and financial support of government is placed behind a particular religious belief, the indirect coercive pressure upon religious minorities to conform to the prevailing officially approved religion is plain."

. . . . When government, the Court said, allies itself with one particular form of religion, the inevitable result is that it incurs "the hatred, disrespect and even contempt of those who held contrary beliefs."

The wholesome "neutrality" of which this Court's cases speak thus stems from a recognition of the teachings of history that powerful sects or groups might bring about a fusion of governmental and religious functions or a concert or dependency of one upon the other to the end that official support of the State or Federal Government would be placed behind the tenets of one or of all orthodoxies. This the Establishment Clause prohibits. And a further reason for neutrality is found in the Free Exercise Clause, which recognizes the value of religious training, teaching and observance and, more particularly, the right of every person to freely choose his own course with reference thereto, free of any compulsion from the state. This the Free Exercise Clause guarantees. Thus, as we have seen, the two clauses may overlap. . . .

Applying the Establishment Clause principles to [these cases] we find that [Pennsylvania is] requiring the selection and reading at the opening of the school day of verses from the Holy Bible and the recitation of the Lord's Prayer by the students in unison. These exercises are prescribed as part of the curricular activities of students who are required by law to attend school. They are held in the school buildings under the supervision and with the participation of teachers employed in those schools. . . . The trial court [in the Schempp case] has found that such an opening exercise is a religious ceremony and was intended by the State to be so. We agree with the trial court's finding as to the religious character of the exercises. Given that finding, the exercises and the law requiring them are in violation of the Establishment Clause.

There is no such specific finding as to the religious character of the exercises in [the Murray case], and the State contends ... that the program is an effort to extend its benefits to all public school children without regard to their religious belief. Included within its secular purposes, it says, are the promotion of moral values, the contradiction to the materialistic trends of our times, the perpetuation of our institutions and the teaching of literature. The case came up on demurrer [an allegation by a defendant], of course, to a petition which alleged that the uniform practice under the rule had been to read from the King James verion of the Bible and that the exercise was sectarian. The short answer, therefore, is that the religious character of the exercise was admitted by the State. But even if its purpose is not strictly religious, it is sought to be accomplished through readings, without comment, from the Bible. Surely the place of the Bible as an instrument of religion cannot be gainsaid, and the State's recognition of the pervading religious character of the ceremony is evident from the rule's specific permission of the alternative use of the Catholic Douay version as well as the recent amendment permitting nonattendance at the exercises. None of these factors is consistent with the contention that the Bible is here used either as an instrument for nonreligious moral inspiration or as a reference for the teaching of secular subjects.

The conclusion follows that . . . the [law] require[s] religious exercises and such exercises are being conducted in direct violation of the rights of the [Murrays]. Nor are these required exercises mitigated [lessened] by the fact that individual students may absent themselves upon parental request, for that fact furnishes no defense to a claim of unconstitutionality under the Establishment Clause. Further, it is no defense to urge that the religious practices here may be relatively minor encroachments on the First Amendment. The breach of neutrality that is today a trickling stream may all too soon become a raging torrent and, in the words of Madison, "it is proper to take alarm at the first experiment on our liberties."

It is insisted that unless these religious exercises are permitted a "religion of secularism" is established in the schools. We agree of course that the State may not establish a "religion of secularism" in the sense of affirmatively opposing or showing hostility to religion, thus "preferring those who believe in no religion over those who do believe." We do not agree, however, that this decision in any sense has that effect. In addition, it might well be said that one's education is not complete without a study of comparative religion or the history of religion and its relationship to the advancement of civilization. It certainly may be said that the Bible is worthy of study for its literary and historic qualities. Nothing we have said here indicates that such study of the Bible or of religion, when presented objectively as part of a secular program of education, may not be effected consistently with the First Amendment. But the exercise . . . [is a] religious [exercise], required by the [State] in violation of the command of the First Amendment that the Government maintain strict neutrality, neither aiding nor opposing religion.

Finally, we cannot accept that the concept of neutrality, which does not permit a State to require a religious exercise even with the consent of the majority of those affected, collides with the majority's right to free exercise of religion. While the Free Exercise Clause clearly prohibits the use of state action to deny the rights of free exercise to *anyone*, it has never meant that a majority could use the machinery of the State to practice its beliefs. . . .

The place of religion in our society is an exalted one, achieved through a long tradition of reliance on the home, the church and the inviolable citadel of the individual heart and mind. We have come to recognize through bitter experience that it is not within the power of government to invade that citadel, whether its purpose or effect be to aid or oppose, to advance or retard. In the relationship between man and religion, the State is firmly committed to a position of neutrality. Though the application of that rule requires interpretation of a delicate sort, the rule itself is clearly and concisely stated in the words of the First Amendment. Applying that rule to the facts of these cases, we affirm [uphold] the judgment in [Abington v. Schempp]. In [Murray v. Curlett], the judgment is reversed and the cause remanded [sent back] to the Maryland Court of Appeals for further proceedings consistent with this opinion.

It is so ordered.

The "Monkey" Law
Epperson v. Arkansas

If today you can take a thing like evolution and make it a crime to teach in the public school, tomorrow you can make it a crime to teach in the private school.

- **Clarence Darrow**

In 1859 Charles Darwin published *The Origin of Species*, which contained his theory of evolution. In the 1920's several states, including Arkansas, Mississippi, Oklahoma, Texas, and Tennessee, enacted "Monkey Laws," which prohibited the teaching of Darwin's Theory of Evolution. Tennessee's 1925 *Act Prohibiting the Teaching of Evolution* was unsuccessfully challenged in the "Scopes Monkey Trial." Arkansas' 1928 Anti-Evolutionary Act went unchallenged for almost forty years.

Susan Epperson, who held a master's degree in zoology from the University of Illinois, was hired to teach a tenth grade biology class at Little Rock's Central High. In 1965 a new required biology text, which included material on Darwin's Theory of Evolution, was adopted by the Little Rock Schools. The adoption of the new textbook created an impossible situation for Epperson: Arkansas could dismiss her for teaching evolution from a textbook that Arkansas required her to use. Epperson, who wished to teach Darwin's Theory free from state interference, sued, seeking to have the Anti-Evolution Act overturned as a violation of the First Amendment's Religion Clauses.

Arkansas' Chancellery Court struck down the Anti-Evolutionary Act. The Arkansas Supreme Court reversed the lower court. Susan Epperson appealed to the United States Supreme Court.

Oral arguments were heard on October 16, 1968 and the 9-0 decision of the Court was announced on November 12, 1968 by Associate Justice Abe Fortas.

THE EPPERSON COURT

Chief Justice Earl Warren
Appointed Chief Justice by President Eisenhower
Served 1953 - 1969

Associate Justice Hugo Black
Appointed by President Franklin Roosevelt
Served 1937 - 1971

Associate Justice William O. Douglas
Appointed by President Franklin Roosevelt
Served 1939 - 1975

Associate Justice Tom Clark
Appointed by President Truman
Served 1949 - 1967

Associate Justice John Marshall Harlan
Appointed by President Eisenhower
Served 1955 - 1971

Associate Justice William Brennan
Appointed by President Eisenhower
Served 1956 - 1990

Associate Justice Potter Stewart
Appointed by President Eisenhower
Served 1958 - 1981

Associate Justice Byron White
Appointed by President Kennedy
Served 1962 - 1993

Associate Justice Abe Fortas
Appointed by President Johnson
Served 1965 - 1969

The unedited text of *Epperson v. Arkansas* can be found
on page 97, volume 393 of *United States Reports.*

EPPERSON v. ARKANSAS
November 12, 1968

JUSTICE FORTAS: This appeal challenges the constitutionality of the "anti-evolution" statute which the State of Arkansas adopted in 1928 to prohibit the teaching in its public schools and universities of the theory that man evolved from other species of life. The statute was a product of the upsurge of "fundamentalist" religious fervor of the twenties. The Arkansas statute was an adaptation of the famous Tennessee "monkey law" which that State adopted in 1925. The constitutionality of the Tennessee law was upheld by the Tennessee Supreme Court in the celebrated *Scopes* case in 1927.

The Arkansas law makes it unlawful for a teacher in any state-supported school or university "to teach the theory or doctrine that mankind ascended or descended from a lower order of animals," or "to adopt or use in any such institution a textbook that teaches" this theory. Violation is a misdemeanor and subjects the violator to dismissal from his position.

The present case concerns the teaching of biology in a high school in Little Rock. According to the testimony, until the events here in litigation, the official textbook furnished for the high school biology course did not have a section on the Darwinian Theory. Then, for the academic year 1965-1966, the school administration, on recommendation of the teachers of biology in the school system, adopted and prescribed a textbook which contained a chapter setting forth "the theory about the origin . . . of man from a lower form of animal."

Susan Epperson, a young woman who graduated from Arkansas' school system and then obtained her master's degree in zoology at the University of Illinois, was employed by the Little Rock system in the fall of 1964 to teach tenth grade biology at Central High School. At the start of the next academic year, 1965, she was confronted by the new textbook (which one surmises from the record was not unwelcome to her). She faced at least a literal dilemma because she was supposed to use the new textbook for classroom instruction and presumably to teach the statutorily condemned chapter; but to do so would be a criminal offense and subject her to dismissal.

She [went before] the Chancery Court of the State, seeking a declaration that the Arkansas statute is void and enjoining [stopping] the State and the defendant officials of the Little Rock school system from dismissing her for violation of the statute's provisions. H.H. Blanchard, a parent of children attending the public schools, intervened in [her] support. . . .

The Chancery Court, in an opinion by Chancellor Murray O. Reid, held that the statute violated the Fourteenth Amendment to the United States Constitution. The court noted that this Amendment encompasses the prohibitions upon state interference with freedom of speech and thought which are contained in the First Amendment. Accordingly, it held that the challenged statute is unconstitutional because, in violation of the First Amendment, it "tends to hinder the quest for knowledge, restrict the freedom to learn, and restrain the freedom to teach." In this perspective, the Act, it held, was an unconstitutional and void restraint upon the freedom of speech guaranteed by the Constitution.

On appeal, the Supreme Court of Arkansas reversed [this decision. In a] two-sentence opinion . . . [i]t sustained [upheld] the statute as an exercise of the State's power to specify the curriculum in public schools. It did not address itself to the . . . constitutional [questions].

Appeal was [made] to this Court. . . . Only Arkansas and Mississippi have . . . "anti-evolution" or "monkey" laws on their books. There is no record of any prosecutions in Arkansas under its statute. It is possible that the statute is presently more of a curiosity than a vital fact of life in these States. Nevertheless . . . it is our duty to decide the issues presented.

At the outset, it is urged upon us that the challenged statute is vague and uncertain and therefore within the condemnation of the Due Process Clause of the Fourteenth Amendment. The contention that the Act is vague and uncertain is supported by language in the brief opinion of Arkansas' Supreme Court. That court, perhaps reflecting the discomfort which the statute's quixotic prohibition necessarily engenders in the modern mind, stated that it "expresses no opinion" as to whether the Act prohibits "explanation" of the theory of evolution or merely forbids "teaching that the theory is true." Regardless of this uncertainty, the court held that the statute is constitutional.

On the other hand, counsel for the State, in oral argument in this Court, candidly stated that, despite the State Supreme Court's equivocation, Arkansas would interpret the statute "to mean that to make a student aware of the theory . . . just to teach that there was such a theory" would be grounds for dismissal and for prosecution under the statute; and he said "that the Supreme Court of

Arkansas' opinion should be interpreted in that manner."
He said: "If Mrs. Epperson would tell her students that
'Here is Darwin's theory, that man ascended or descended
from a lower form of being,' then I think she would be
under this statute liable for prosecution."

In any event, we do not rest our decision upon the
asserted vagueness of the statute. On either interpretation
of its language, Arkansas' statute cannot stand. It is of no
moment whether the law is deemed to prohibit mention of
Darwin's theory, or to forbid any or all of the infinite
varieties of communication embraced within the term
"teaching." Under either interpretation, the law must be
stricken because of its conflict with the constitutional
prohibition of state laws respecting an establishment of
religion or prohibiting the free exercise thereof. The
overriding fact is that Arkansas' law selects from the
body of knowledge a particular segment which it
proscribes for the sole reason that it is deemed to conflict
with a particular religious doctrine; that is, with a
particular interpretation of the Book of Genesis by a
particular religious group.

The antecedents of today's decision are many and
unmistakable. They are rooted in the foundation soil of
our Nation. They are fundamental to freedom.

Government in our democracy, state and national, must be
neutral in matters of religious theory, doctrine, and
practice. It may not be hostile to any religion or to the
advocacy of no-religion; and it may not aid, foster, or
promote one religion or religious theory against another
or even against the militant opposite. The First

Amendment mandates governmental neutrality between religion and religion, and between religion and nonreligion.

As early as 1872, this Court said: "The law knows no heresy, and is committed to the support of no dogma, the establishment of no sect." This has been the interpretation of the great First Amendment which this Court has applied in the many and subtle problems which the ferment of our national life has presented for decision within the Amendment's broad command.

Judicial [intrusion] in the operation of the public school system of the Nation raises problems requiring care and restraint. Our courts, however, have not failed to apply the First Amendment's mandate [rule] in our educational system where [it is] essential to safeguard the fundamental values of freedom of speech and inquiry and of belief. By and large, public education in our Nation is committed to the control of state and local authorities. Courts do not and cannot intervene in the resolution of conflicts which arise in the daily operation of school systems and which do not directly and sharply implicate basic constitutional values. On the other hand, "[t]he vigilant protection of constitutional freedoms is nowhere more vital than in the community of American schools." As this Court said in *Keyishian v. Board of Regents*, the First Amendment "does not tolerate laws that cast a pall of orthodoxy over the classroom."

The earliest cases in this Court on the subject of the impact of constitutional guarantees upon the classroom were decided before the Court expressly applied the specific prohibitions of the First Amendment to the States. But as early as 1923, the Court did not hesitate to condemn under the Due Process Clause "arbitrary" restrictions upon the freedom of teachers to teach and of students to learn. In that year, the Court, in an opinion by Justice McReynolds [in *Meyer v. Nebraska*], held unconstitutional an Act of the State of Nebraska making it a crime to teach any subject in any language other than English to pupils who had not passed the eighth grade. The State's purpose in enacting the law was to promote civic cohesiveness by encouraging the learning of English and to combat the "baneful effect" of permitting foreigners to rear and educate their children in the language of the parents' native land. The Court recognized these purposes, and it acknowledged the State's power to prescribe the school curriculum, but it held that these were not adequate to support the restriction upon the liberty of teacher and pupil. The challenged statute, it held, unconstitutionally interfered with the right of the individual, guaranteed by the Due Process Clause, to engage in any of the common occupations of life and to acquire useful knowledge.

For purposes of the present case, we need not re-enter the difficult terrain which the Court, in 1923, traversed without apparent misgivings. We need not take advantage of the broad premise which the Court's decision in *Meyer* furnishes, nor need we explore the implications of that decision in terms of the justiciability of the multitude of controversies that beset our campuses today. Today's problem is capable of resolution in the narrower terms of the First Amendment's prohibition of laws respecting an establishment of religion or prohibiting the free exercise thereof.

There is and can be no doubt that the First Amendment does not permit the State to require that teaching and learning must be tailored to the principles or prohibitions of any religious sect or dogma. In *Everson v. Board of Education*, this Court, in upholding a state law to provide free bus service to school children, including those attending parochial schools, said: "Neither [a State nor the Federal Government] can pass laws which aid one religion, aid all religions, or prefer one religion, or prefer one religion over another."

At the following Term of Court, in *McCollum v. Board of Education*, the Court held that Illinois could not release pupils from class to attend classes of instruction in the school buildings in the religion of their choice. This, it said, would involve the State in using tax-supported property for religious purposes, thereby breaching the "wall of separation" which, according to Jefferson, the First Amendment was intended to erect between church and state. While study of religions and of the Bible from a literary and historic viewpoint, presented objectively as part of a secular program of education, need not collide with the First Amendment's prohibition, the State may not adopt programs or practices in its public schools or colleges which "aid or oppose" any religion. This prohibition is absolute. It forbids alike the preference of a religious doctrine or the prohibition of theory which is deemed antagonistic to a particular dogma. As Justice Clark stated in *Joseph Burstyn, Inc. v. Wilson*, "the state has no legitimate interest in protecting any or all religions from views distasteful to them. . . ." The test was stated as follows in *Abington School District v. Schempp*, "[W]hat are the purpose and the primary effect of the enactment? If either is the advancement or inhibition of religion then the enactment exceeds the scope of legislative power as circumscribed by the Constitution."

These precedents inevitably determine the result in the present case. The State's undoubted right to prescribe the curriculum for its public schools does not carry with it the right to prohibit, on pain of criminal penalty, the teaching of a scientific theory or doctrine where that prohibition is based upon reasons that violate the First Amendment. It is much too late to argue that the State may impose upon the teachers in its schools any conditions that it chooses, however restrictive they may be of constitutional guarantees.

In the present case, there can be no doubt that Arkansas has sought to prevent its teachers from discussing the theory of evolution because it is contrary to the belief of some that the Book of Genesis must be the exclusive source of doctrine as to the origin of man. No suggestion has been made that Arkansas' law may be justified by considerations of state policy other than the religious views of some of its citizens. It is clear that fundamentalist sectarian conviction was and is the law's reason for existence. Its antecedent, Tennessee's "monkey law," candidly stated its purpose: to make it unlawful "to teach any theory that denies the story of the Divine Creation of man as taught in the Bible, and to teach instead that man has descended from a lower order of animals." Perhaps the sensational publicity attendant upon the *Scopes* trial induced Arkansas to adopt less explicit language. It eliminated Tennessee's reference to "the story of the Divine Creation of man" as taught in the Bible, but there is no doubt that the motivation for the law was the same: to suppress the teaching of a theory which, it was thought, "denied" the divine creation of man. Arkansas' law cannot be defended as an act of religious neutrality. Arkansas did not seek to excise from the curricula of its schools and universities all discussion of the origin of man. The law's effort was confined to an attempt to blot out a particular theory because of its supposed conflict with the Biblical account, literally read. Plainly, the law is contrary to the mandate of the First, and in violation of the Fourteenth, Amendment to the Constitution.

The judgment of the Supreme Court of Arkansas is reversed.

Tax Exemptions For Church Property
Walz v. New York Tax Commission

Real property owned by a group organized exclusively for religious purposes and used exclusively for carrying out of such purposes, shall be exempt from taxation.

- New York State's Church Property Tax Exemption Law

The New York State Constitution provided for a tax exemption for real property used for religious purposes. The exemption of church property from taxation, authorized by the State Constitution, was implemented by New York's Church Property Tax Exemption Law.

Fredrick Walz, an owner of non-exempt real property in New York State, challenged the constitutional validity of New York State's Church Property Tax Exemption Law. Walz brought suit in the New York Courts against the Tax Commission of the City of New York to prevent the Commission from granting, under the Church Property Tax Exemption Law, property tax exemptions to religious organizations. Walz argued that New York's granting of tax exemptions for church property indirectly required him, and all other owners of non-tax exempt property, to make contributions, in the form of higher property taxes, to tax exempt religious organizations. Walz argued that this constituted a violation of the First Amendment's Establishment Clause.

A New York trial court upheld the Church Property Tax Exemption Law. The Appellate Division of the New York State Supreme Court and the New York Court of Appeals upheld the trial court. Walz appealed to the United States Supreme Court.

Oral arguments were heard on November 19, 1969 and the 8-1 decision of the Court was announced on May 4, 1970 by Chief Justice Warren Burger.

THE WALZ COURT

Chief Justice Warren Burger
Appointed Chief Justice by President Nixon
Served 1969 - 1986

Associate Justice Hugo Black
Appointed by President Franklin Roosevelt
Served 1937 - 1971

Associate Justice William O. Douglas
Appointed by President Franklin Roosevelt
Served 1939 - 1975

Associate Justice John Marshall Harlan
Appointed by President Eisenhower
Served 1955 - 1971

Associate Justice William Brennan
Appointed by President Eisenhower
Served 1956 - 1990

Associate Justice Potter Stewart
Appointed by President Eisenhower
Served 1958 - 1981

Associate Justice Byron White
Appointed by President Kennedy
Served 1962 - 1993

Associate Justice Thurgood Marshall
Appointed by President Lyndon Johnson
Served 1967 - 1991

Associate Justice Harry Blackmun
Appointed by President Nixon
Served 1970 - 1994

The unedited text of *Walz v. New York Tax Commission* can be found on page 664, volume 397 of *United States Reports.*

WALZ v. NEW YORK CITY
TAX COMMISSION
May 4, 1970

CHIEF JUSTICE BURGER: Appellant [Walz], owner of real estate in Richmond County, New York, sought an injunction [a court order stopping an action] in the New York courts to prevent the New York City Tax Commission from granting property tax exemptions to religious organizations for religious properties used solely for religious worship. The exemption from state taxes is authorized by . . . the New York Constitution, which provides in relevant part:

> "Exemptions from taxation may be granted only by general laws. Exemptions may be altered or repealed except those exempting real or personal property used exclusively for religious, educational or charitable purposes as defined by law and owned by any corporation or association organized or conducted exclusively for one or more of such purposes and not operating for profit."

The essence of [Walz'] contention was that the New York City Tax Commission's grant of an exemption to church property indirectly requires [Walz] to make a contribution to religious bodies and thereby violates provisions prohibiting establishment of religion under the First Amendment which under the Fourteenth Amendment is binding on the States.

[The Tax Commission]'s motion for summary judgment [questioning of a material fact] was granted and the Appellate Division of the New York Supreme Court, and the

New York Court of Appeals affirmed [upheld]. We [also] affirm.

Prior opinions of this Court have discussed the development and historical background of the First Amendment in detail. It would therefore serve no useful purpose to review in detail the background of the Establishment and Free Exercise Clauses of the First Amendment or to restate what the Court's opinions have reflected over the years.

It is sufficient to note that for the men who wrote the Religion Clauses of the First Amendment the "establishment" of a religion connoted sponsorship, financial support, and active involvement of the sovereign in religious activity. . . .

The Establishment and Free Exercise Clauses of the First Amendment are not the most precisely drawn portions of the Constitution. The sweep of the absolute prohibitions in the Religion Clauses may have been calculated; but the purpose was to state an objective, not to write a statute. In attempting to articulate the scope of the two Religion Clauses, the Court's opinions reflect the limitations inherent in formulating general principles on a case-by-case basis. The considerable internal inconsistency in the opinions of the Court derives from what, in retrospect, may have been too sweeping utterances on aspects of these clauses that seemed clear in relation to the particular cases but have limited meaning as general principles.

The Court has struggled to find a neutral course between the two Religion Clauses, both of which are cast in absolute terms, and either of which, if expanded to a logical extreme, would tend to clash with the other. . . .

With all the risks inherent in programs that bring about administrative relationships between public education bodies and church-sponsored schools, we have been able to chart a course that preserved the autonomy and freedom of religious bodies while avoiding any semblance of established religion. This is a "tight rope" and one we have successfully traversed.

The legislative purpose of the property tax exemption is neither the advancement nor the inhibition of religion; it is neither sponsorship nor hostility. New York, in common with the other States, has determined that certain entities that exist in a harmonious relationship to the community at large, and that foster its "moral or mental improvement," should not be inhibited in their activities by property taxation or the hazard of loss of those properties for nonpayment of taxes. It has not singled out one particular church or religious group or even churches as such; rather, it has granted exemption to all houses of religious worship within a broad class of property owned by nonprofit, quasi-public corporations which include hospitals, libraries, playgrounds, scientific, professional, historical, and patriotic groups. The State has an affirmative policy that considers these groups as beneficial and stabilizing influences in community life and finds this classification useful, desirable, and in the public interest. Qualification for tax exemption is not perpetual or immutable; some tax-exempt groups lose that status when their activities take them outside the classification and new entities can come into being and qualify for exemption.

Governments have not always been tolerant of religious activity, and hostility toward religion has taken many shapes and forms - economic, political, and sometimes harshly oppressive. Grants of exemption historically reflect the concern of authors of constitutions and statutes as to the latent dangers inherent in the imposition of property taxes; exemption constitutes a reasonable and balanced attempt to guard against those dangers. The limits of permissible state accommodation to religion are by no means co-extensive with the noninterference mandated by the Free Exercise Clause. To equate the two would be to deny a national heritage with roots in the Revolution itself. We cannot read New York's statute as attempting to establish religion; it is simply sparing the exercise of religion from the burden of property taxation levied on private profit institutions.

We find it unnecessary to justify the tax exemption on the social welfare services or "good works" that some churches perform for parishioners and others - family counselling, aid to the elderly and the infirm, and to children. Churches vary substantially in the scope of such services; programs expand or contract according to resources and need. As public-sponsored programs enlarge, private aid from the church sector may diminish. The extent of social services may vary, depending on whether the church serves an urban or rural, a rich or poor constituency. To give emphasis to so variable an aspect of the work of religious bodies would introduce an element of governmental evaluation and standards as to the worth of particular social welfare programs, thus producing a kind of continuing day-to-day relationship which the policy of neutrality seeks to minimize. Hence, the use of a social welfare yardstick as a significant element to qualify for tax exemption could conceivably give rise to confrontations that could escalate to constitutional dimensions.

Determining that the legislative purpose of tax exemption is not aimed at establishing, sponsoring, or supporting religion does not end the inquiry, however. We must also be sure that the end result - the effect - is not an excessive government entanglement with religion. The test is inescapably one of degree. Either course, taxation of churches or exemption, occasions some degree of involvement with religion. Elimination of exemption would tend to expand the involvement of government by giving rise to tax valuation of church property, tax liens, tax foreclosures, and the direct confrontations and conflicts that follow in the train of those legal processes.

Granting tax exemptions to churches necessarily operates to afford an indirect economic benefit and also gives rise to some, but yet a lesser, involvement than taxing them. In analyzing either alternative the questions are whether the involvement is excessive, and whether it is a continuing one calling for official and continuing surveillance leading to an impermissible degree of entanglement. Obviously a direct money subsidy would be a relationship pregnant with involvement and, as with most governmental grant programs, could encompass sustained and detailed administrative relationships for enforcement of statutory or administrative standards, but that is not this case. The hazards of churches supporting government are hardly less in their potential than the hazards of government supporting churches; each relationship carries some involvement rather than the desired insulation and separation. We cannot ignore the instances in history when church support of government led to the kind of involvement we seek to avoid.

The grant of a tax exemption is not sponsorship since the government does not transfer part of its revenue to churches but simply abstains from demanding that the church support the state. No one has ever suggested that tax exemption has converted libraries, art galleries, or hospitals into arms of the state or put employees "on the public payroll." There is no genuine nexus between tax exemption and establishment of religion. As Justice Holmes commented in a related context "a page of history is worth a volume of logic." The exemption creates only a minimal and remote involvement between church and state and far less than taxation of churches. It restricts the fiscal relationship between church and state, and tends to complement and reinforce the desired separation insulating each from the other.

Separation in this context cannot mean absence of all contact; the complexities of modern life inevitably produce some contact and the fire and police protection received by houses of religious worship are no more than incidental benefits accorded all persons or institutions within a State's boundaries, along with many other exempt organizations. [Walz] has not established even an arguable quantitative correlation between the payment of [a] property tax and the receipt of these municipal benefits.

All of the fifty States provide for tax exemptions of places of worship, most of them doing so by constitutional guarantees. For so long as federal income taxes have had any potential impact on churches - over seventy-five years - religious organizations have been expressly exempt from the tax. Such treatment is an "aid" to churches no more and no less in principle than the real estate tax exemption granted by States. Few concepts are more deeply embedded in the fabric of our national life, beginning with pre-Revolutionary colonial times, than for the government to exercise at the very least this kind of benevolent neutrality toward churches and religious exercise generally so long as none was favored over others and none suffered interference.

It is significant that Congress, from its earliest days, has viewed the Religion Clauses of the Constitution as authorizing statutory real estate tax exemption to religious bodies. . . .

Nothing in this national attitude toward religious tolerance and two centuries of uninterrupted freedom from taxation has given the remotest sign of leading to an established church or religion and on the contrary it has operated affirmatively to help guarantee the free exercise of all forms of religious belief. . . .

It is interesting to note that while the precise question we now decide has not been directly before the Court previously, the broad question was discussed by the Court in relation to real estate taxes assessed nearly a century ago on land owned by and adjacent to a church in Washington, D.C. At that time Congress granted real estate tax exemptions to buildings devoted to art, to institutions of public charity, libraries, cemeteries, and "church buildings, and grounds actually occupied by such buildings." In denying tax exemption as to land owned by but not used for the church, but rather to produce income, the Court concluded:

> "In the exercise of this [taxing] power, Congress, like any State legislature unrestricted by constitutional provisions, may at its discretion wholly exempt certain classes of property from taxation, or may tax them at a lower rate than other property."

It appears that at least up to 1885 this Court, reflecting more than a century of our history and uninterrupted practice, accepted without discussion the proposition that federal or state grants of tax exemption to churches were not a violation of the Religion Clauses of the First Amendment. As to the New York statute, we now confirm that view.

Affirmed.

Taxpayer Support Of Religious Schools
Lemon v Kurtzman/Robinson v DiCenso

The same authority which can force a citizen to contribute three pence of his property for the support of a religion may force him to conform to that religion.

- James Madison

In 1968 Pennsylvania enacted *The Non-Public Elementary and Secondary Education Act,* authorizing the Superintendent of Public Instruction to reimburse the State's parochial schools for secular teaching costs. A taxpayer, Alton Lemon, sued David Kurtzman, the State Superintendent of Public Instruction, asserting that the Pennsylvania Act violated the First Amendment's Establishment of Religion and Free Exercise of Religion Clauses. The U.S. District Court for Pennsylvania found for Kurtzman, holding that the Act was not a violation of the Constitution. Lemon appealed to the United States Supreme Court.

In 1969 Rhode Island enacted *The Non-Public School Teachers Salary Supplement Act* authorizing the Commissioner of Education to supplement the salaries of teachers of secular subjects in the States' parochial schools. A taxpayer, Joan DiCenso, sued William Robinson, the State Commissioner of Education, asserting that the Rhode Island Act violated the First Amendment's Establishment of Religion and Free Exercise of Religion Clauses. The U.S. District Court for Rhode Island found for DiCenso, holding that the Act was a violation of the Constitution. Robinson appealed to the United States Supreme Court.

Appeals from the contrary decisions of the Pennsylvania and Rhode Island Federal District Courts were combined. Oral arguments were heard on March 3, 1971; the 8-0 (*Lemon v. Kurtzman*) and 8-1 (*Robinson v. DiCenso*) decisions of the Court were announced on June 28, 1971 by Chief Justice Warren Burger.

THE LEMON/ROBINSON COURT

Chief Justice Warren Burger
Appointed Chief Justice by President Nixon
Served 1969 - 1986

Associate Justice Hugo Black
Appointed by President Franklin Roosevelt
Served 1937 - 1971

Associate Justice William O. Douglas
Appointed by President Franklin Roosevelt
Served 1939 - 1975

Associate Justice John Marshall Harlan
Appointed by President Eisenhower
Served 1955 - 1971

Associate Justice William Brennan
Appointed by President Eisenhower
Served 1956 -1990

Associate Justice Potter Stewart
Appointed by President Eisenhower
Served 1958 - 1981

Associate Justice Byron White
Appointed by President Kennedy
Served 1962 - 1993

Associate Justice Thurgood Marshall
Appointed by President Lyndon Johnson
Served 1967 - 1991

Associate Justice Harry Blackmun
Appointed by President Nixon
Served 1970 - 1994

The unedited text of *Lemon v. Kurtzman* and *Robinson v. DiCenso* can be found on page 602, volume 403 of *United States Reports*.

LEMON v. KURTZMAN
ROBINSON v. DiCENSO
June 28, 1971

CHIEF JUSTICE BURGER: These two appeals raise questions as to Pennsylvania and Rhode Island statutes providing state aid to church-related elementary and secondary schools. Both statutes are challenged as violative of the Establishment and Free Exercise Clauses of the First Amendment and the Due Process Clause of the Fourteenth Amendment.

Pennsylvania has adopted a statutory program that provides financial support to nonpublic elementary and secondary schools by way of reimbursement for the cost of teachers' salaries, textbooks, and instructional materials in specified secular subjects. Rhode Island has adopted a statute under which the State pays directly to teachers in nonpublic elementary schools a supplement of fifteen percent of their annual salary. Under each statute state aid has been given to church-related educational institutions. We hold that both statutes are unconstitutional.

.... In *Everson v. Board of Education*, this Court upheld a state statute that reimbursed the parents of parochial school children for bus transportation expenses. There Justice Black, writing for the majority, suggested that the decision carried to "the verge" of forbidden territory under the Religion Clauses. Candor compels acknowledgment, moreover, that we can only dimly perceive the lines of demarcation in this extraordinarily sensitive area of constitutional law.

The language of the Religion Clauses of the First Amendment is at best opaque, particularly when compared with other portions of the Amendment. Its authors did not simply prohibit the establishment of a state church or a state religion, an area history shows they regarded as very important and fraught with great dangers. Instead they commanded that there should be "no law *respecting* an establishment of religion." A law may be one "respecting" the forbidden objective while falling short of its total realization. A law "respecting" the proscribed result, that is, the establishment of religion, is not always easily identifiable as one violative of the Clause. A given law might not *establish* a state religion but nevertheless be one "respecting" that end in the sense of being a step that could lead to such establishment and hence offend the First Amendment.

In the absence of precisely stated constitutional prohibitions, we must draw lines with reference to the three main evils against which the Establishment Clause was intended to afford protection: "sponsorship, financial support, and active involvement of the sovereign in religious activity."

Every analysis in this area must begin with consideration of the cumulative criteria developed by the Court over many years. Three such tests may be gleaned from our cases. First, the statute must have a secular legislative purpose; second, its principal or primary effect must be one that neither advances nor inhibits religion; finally, the statute must not foster "an excessive government entanglement with religion."

.... [W]e conclude that the cumulative impact of the entire relationship arising under the statutes in each State involves excessive entanglement between government and religion.

. . . . Our prior holdings do not call for total separation between church and state; total separation is not possible in an absolute sense. Some relationship between government and religious organizations is inevitable. . . . Judicial caveats against entanglement must recognize that the line of separation, far from being a "wall," is a blurred, indistinct, and variable barrier depending on all the circumstances of a particular relationship.

This is not to suggest, however, that we are to engage in a legalistic minuet in which precise rules and forms must govern. A true minuet is a matter of pure form and style, the observance of which is itself the substantive end. Here we examine the form of the relationship for the light that it casts on the substance.

In order to determine whether the government entanglement with religion is excessive, we must examine the character and purposes of the institutions that are benefited, the nature of the aid that the State provides, and the resulting relationship between the government and the religious authority. Justice Harlan, in a separate opinion in *Walz*, echoed the classic warning as to "programs, whose very nature is apt to entangle the state in details of administration. . . ." Here we find that both statutes foster an impermissible degree of entanglement.

. . . . We have no long history of state aid to church-related educational institutions comparable to two hundred years of tax exemption for churches. Indeed, the state programs before us today represent something of an innovation. We have already noted that modern governmental programs have self-perpetuating and self-expanding propensities. These internal pressures are only enhanced when the schemes involve institutions whose legitimate needs are growing and whose interests have substantial political support. Nor can we fail to see that in constitutional adjudication some steps, which when taken were thought to approach "the verge," have become the platform for yet further steps. A certain momentum develops in constitutional theory and it can be a "downhill thrust" easily set in motion but difficult to retard or stop. Development by momentum is not invariably bad; indeed, it is the way the common law has grown, but it is a force to be recognized and reckoned with. The dangers are increased by the difficulty of perceiving in advance exactly where the "verge" of the precipice lies. As well as constituting an independent evil against which the Religion Clauses were intended to protect, involvement or entanglement between government and religion serves as a warning signal.

Finally, nothing we have said can be construed [interpreted] to disparage the role of church-related elementary and secondary schools in our national life. Their contribution has been and is enormous. Nor do we ignore their economic plight in a period of rising costs and expanding need. Taxpayers generally have been spared vast sums by the maintenance of these educational institutions by religious organizations, largely by the gifts of faithful adherents.

The merit and benefits of these schools, however, are not the issue before us in these cases. The sole question is whether state aid to these schools can be squared with the dictates of the Religion Clauses. Under our system the choice has been made that government is to be entirely excluded from the area of religious instruction and churches excluded from the affairs of government. The Constitution decrees that religion must be a private matter for the individual, the family, and the institutions of private choice, and that while some involvement and entanglement are inevitable, lines must be drawn.

The judgment of the Rhode Island District Court . . . is affirmed [upheld]. The judgment of the Pennsylvania District Court . . . is reversed, and the case is remanded [sent back to the lower court] for further proceedings consistent with this opinion.

Compulsory Education Of The Amish
Wisconsin v. Yoder

Unless the child has a legal excuse or has graduated from high school, any person having under his control a child between the ages of seven and sixteen years shall cause such child to attend school regularly.
- Wisconsin's Compulsory Education Law

Wisconsin's Compulsory Education Law required all parents of children seven to sixteen years of age to send their children to a public or private school.

Three Amish families from Green County, Wisconsin - the Yoders, whose daughter Frieda was fifteen, the Millers, whose daughter Barbara was fifteen, and the Yutzys, whose son Vernon was fourteen - refused, on religious grounds, to comply with Wisconsin's Compulsory Education Law. The Yoders and Millers were members of the Old Order Amish Church. The Yutzys were members of the Conservative Amish Mennonite Church. All three families believed that their children's attendance in any school after the eight grade was contrary to their sincerely held Amish beliefs.

The fathers of these three Amish children: Jonas Yoder, Wallace Miller, and Adin Yutzy were tried and convicted in Wisconsin's Green County Court of violating the State's Compulsory Education Law. The three Amish fathers appealed their convictions, based on the First Amendment's Free Exercise Clause, first to the Wisconsin Circuit Court, which upheld their convictions, and then to the Wisconsin Supreme Court, which reversed their convictions. The State of Wisconsin appealed to the United States Supreme Court.

Oral arguments were heard on December 8, 1971 and the 6-1 decision of the Court was announced on May 15, 1972 by Chief Justice Warren Burger.

THE YODER COURT

Chief Justice Warren Burger
Appointed Chief Justice by President Nixon
Served 1969 - 1986

Associate Justice William O. Douglas
Appointed by President Franklin Roosevelt
Served 1939 - 1975

Associate Justice William Brennan
Appointed by President Eisenhower
Served 1956 - 1990

Associate Justice Potter Stewart
Appointed by President Eisenhower
Served 1958 - 1981

Associate Justice Byron White
Appointed by President Kennedy
Served 1962 - 1993

Associate Justice Thurgood Marshall
Appointed by President Lyndon Johnson
Served 1967 - 1991

Associate Justice Harry Blackmun
Appointed by President Nixon
Served 1970 - 1994

The unedited text of *Wisconsin v. Yoder* can be found on page 205, volume 406 of *United States Reports.*

WISCONSIN v. YODER
May 15, 1972

CHIEF JUSTICE BURGER: On [request] of the State of Wisconsin, we [agreed] to review a decision of the Wisconsin Supreme Court holding that respondents' [Yoder, Miller, and Yutzy's] convictions of violating the State's compulsory school-attendance law were invalid under the Free Exercise Clause of the First Amendment to the United States Constitution made applicable to the States by the Fourteenth Amendment. For the reasons hereafter stated we affirm [uphold] the judgment of the Supreme Court of Wisconsin.

. . . Jonas Yoder and Wallace Miller are members of the Old Order Amish religion, and . . . Adin Yutzy is a member of the Conservative Amish Mennonite Church. They and their families are residents of Green County, Wisconsin. Wisconsin's compulsory school-attendance law required them to [send] their children to . . . public or private school until reaching age sixteen but [they] declined to send their children, ages fourteen and fifteen, to public school after they completed the eighth grade. The children were not enrolled in any private school, or within any recognized exception to the compulsory-attendance law, and they are conceded to be subject to the Wisconsin statute.

On complaint of the school district administrator for the public schools, [Yoder, Miller, and Yutzy] were charged, tried, and convicted of violating the compulsory-attendance law in Green County Court and were fined the sum of $5 each. [Yoder, Miller, and Yutzy] defended on the ground that the application of the compulsory-attendance law violated their rights under the First and

Fourteenth Amendments. The trial testimony showed that [they] believed, in accordance with the tenets of Old Order Amish communities generally, that their children's attendance at high school, public or private, was contrary to the Amish religion and way of life. They believed that by sending their children to high school, they would not only expose themselves to the danger of the censure of the church community, but, as found by the county court, also endanger their own salvation and that of their children. The State stipulated [agreed] that [Yoder, Miller, and Yutzy's] religious beliefs were sincere.

. . . . Amish objection to formal education beyond the eighth grade is firmly grounded in the[ir] central religious concepts. They object to the high school, and higher education generally, because the values they teach are in marked variance with Amish values and the Amish way of life; they view secondary school education as an impermissible exposure of their children to a "worldly" influence in conflict with their beliefs. The high school tends to emphasize intellectual and scientific accomplishments, self-distinction, competitiveness, worldly success, and social life with other students. Amish society emphasizes informal learning-through-doing; a life of "goodness," rather than a life of intellect; wisdom, rather than technical knowledge; community welfare, rather than competition; and separation from, rather than integration with, contemporary worldly society.

Formal high school education beyond the eighth grade is contrary to Amish beliefs, not only because it places Amish children in an environment hostile to Amish beliefs with increasing emphasis on competition in class work and sports and with pressure to conform to the styles, manners, and ways of the peer group, but also because it takes them away from their community, physically and emotionally, during the crucial and formative adolescent period of life. During this period, the children must acquire Amish attitudes favoring manual work and self-reliance and the specific skills needed to perform the adult role of an Amish farmer or housewife. They must learn to enjoy physical labor. Once a child has learned basic reading, writing, and elementary mathematics, these traits, skills, and attitudes admittedly fall within the category of those best learned through example and "doing" rather than in a classroom. And, at this time in life, the Amish child must also grow in his faith and his relationship to the Amish community if he is to be prepared to accept the heavy obligations imposed by adult baptism. In short, high school attendance with teachers who are not of the Amish faith - and may even be hostile to it - interposes a serious barrier to the integration of the Amish child into the Amish religious community. . . .

The Amish do not object to elementary education through the first eight grades as a general proposition because they agree that their children must have basic skills in the "three R's" in order to read the Bible, to be good farmers and citizens, and to be able to deal with non-Amish people when necessary in the course of daily affairs. They view such a basic education as acceptable because it does not significantly expose their children to worldly values or interfere with their development in the Amish community during the crucial adolescent period. While Amish accept compulsory elementary education generally, wherever possible they have established their own elementary schools in many respects like the small local schools of the past. In the Amish belief higher learning tends to develop values they reject as influences that alienate man from God.

.... [I]n order for Wisconsin to compel school attendance beyond the eighth grade against a claim that such attendance interferes with the practice of a legitimate religious belief, it must appear either that the State does not deny the free exercise of religious belief by its requirement, or that there is a state interest of sufficient magnitude to override the interest claiming protection under the Free Exercise Clause. ...

A way of life, however virtuous and admirable, may not be interposed as a barrier to reasonable state regulation of education if it is based on purely secular considerations; to have the protection of the Religion Clauses, the claims must be rooted in religious belief. Although a determination of what is a "religious" belief or practice entitled to constitutional protection may present a most delicate question, the very concept of ordered liberty precludes allowing every person to make his own standards on matters of conduct in which society as a whole has important interests. Thus, if the Amish asserted their claims because of their subjective evaluation and rejection of the contemporary secular values accepted by the majority, much as Thoreau rejected the social values of his time and isolated himself at Walden Pond, their claims would not rest on a religious basis. Thoreau's choice was philosophical and personal rather than religious, and such belief does not rise to the demands of the Religion Clauses.

Giving no weight to such secular considerations, however, we see that the record in this case abundantly supports the claim that the traditional way of life of the Amish is not merely a matter of personal preference, but one of deep religious conviction, shared by an organized group, and intimately related to daily living. ...

So long as compulsory education laws were confined to eight grades of elementary basic education imparted in a nearby rural schoolhouse, with a large proportion of students of the Amish faith, the Old Order Amish had little basis to fear that school attendance would expose their children to the worldly influence they reject. But modern compulsory secondary education in rural areas is now largely carried on in a consolidated school, often remote from the student's home and alien to his daily home life. As the record so strongly shows, the values and programs of the modern secondary school are in sharp conflict with the fundamental mode of life mandated by the Amish religion; modern laws requiring compulsory secondary education have accordingly engendered great concern and conflict. The conclusion is inescapable that secondary schooling, by exposing Amish children to worldly influences in terms of attitudes, goals, and values contrary to beliefs, and by substantially interfering with the religious development of the Amish child and his integration into the way of life of the Amish faith community at the crucial adolescent stage of development, contravenes the basic religious tenets and practice of the Amish faith, both as to the parent and the child.

The impact of the compulsory-attendance law on [Yoder, Miller, and Yutzy's] practice of the Amish religion is not only severe, but inescapable, for the Wisconsin law affirmatively compels them, under threat of criminal sanction, to perform acts undeniably at odds with fundamental tenets of their religious beliefs. Nor is the impact of the compulsory-attendance law confined to grave interference with important Amish religious tenets from a subjective point of view. It carries with it precisely the kind of objective danger to the free exercise of religion that the First Amendment was designed to prevent. As the record shows, compulsory school attendance to age sixteen for Amish children carries with it a very real threat of undermining the Amish community and religious practice as they exist today; they must either abandon belief and be assimilated into society at large, or be forced to migrate to some other and more tolerant region.

In sum, the unchallenged testimony of acknowledged experts in education and religious history, almost three hundred years of consistent practice, and strong evidence of a sustained faith pervading and regulating [Yoder, Miller, and Yutzy's] entire mode of life support the claim that enforcement of the State's requirement of compulsory formal education after the eighth grade would gravely endanger if not destroy the free exercise of [their] religious beliefs.

. . . . For the reasons stated we hold, with the Supreme Court of Wisconsin, that the First and Fourteenth Amendments prevent the State from compelling [Yoder, Miller, and Yutzy] to cause their children to attend formal high school to age sixteen. . . .

Aided by a history of three centuries as an identifiable religious sect and a long history as a successful and self-sufficient segment of American society, the Amish in this case have convincingly demonstrated the sincerity of their religious beliefs, the interrelationship of belief with their mode of life, the vital role that belief and daily conduct play in the continued survival of Old Order Amish communities and their religious organization, and the hazards presented by the State's enforcement of a statute generally valid as to others. Beyond this, they have carried the even more difficult burden of demonstrating the adequacy of their alternative mode of continuing informal vocational education in terms of precisely those overall interests that the State advances in support of its program of compulsory high school education. In light of this convincing showing, one that probably few other religious groups or sects could make, and weighing the minimal difference between what the State would require and what the Amish already accept, it was incumbent on the State to show with more particularity how its admittedly strong interest in compulsory education would be adversely affected by granting an exemption to the Amish.

. . . . Affirmed.

The "Ten Commandments" Act
Stone v. Graham

It shall be the duty of the Superintendent of Public Instruction to ensure that a copy of the Ten Commandments shall be displayed on a wall in each public school.
-Kentucky's Ten Commandments Act

Effective June 17, 1978 the Legislature of Kentucky ordered that copies of the Ten Commandments, purchased with private funds to be collected by the State, be posted on the walls of every public elementary and secondary school in the State.

The Kentucky Legislature stated that their purpose in passing the "Ten Commandments Act" was secular, not religious, in nature. In small print below the Ten Commandments there was to appear the following statement:

> The secular application of the Ten Commandments is clearly seen in its adoption as the fundamental legal code of Western Civilization and the Common Law of the United States.

Sydell Stone, a Kentucky citizen, sued James Graham, Kentucky's Superintendent of Education, in State Court to halt statewide enforcement of the "Ten Commandments Act," claiming that the Act was in fact religious, not secular, in nature, and thus was a violation of the First Amendment's Establishment and Free Exercise Clauses. The Franklin County, Kentucky Court found for Superintendent Graham, upholding the constitutionality of the Act. Stone appealed to the Kentucky Supreme Court, which also upheld the Act. Stone appealed to the United States Supreme Court.

The 5-4 decision of the Court was announced on November 17, 1980 *Per Curiam* (by the Court).

THE "TEN COMMANDMENTS" COURT

Chief Justice Warren Burger
Appointed Chief Justice by President Nixon
Served 1969 - 1986

Associate Justice William Brennan
Appointed by President Eisenhower
Served 1956 - 1990

Associate Justice Potter Stewart
Appointed by President Eisenhower
Served 1958 - 1981

Associate Justice Byron White
Appointed by President Kennedy
Served 1962 - 1993

Associate Justice Thurgood Marshall
Appointed by President Lyndon Johnson
Served 1967 - 1991

Associate Justice Harry Blackmun
Appointed by President Nixon
Served 1970 - 1994

Associate Justice Lewis Powell
Appointed by President Nixon
Served 1971 - 1987

Associate Justice William Rehnquist
Appointed by President Nixon
Served 1971 -

Associate Justice John Paul Stevens
Appointed by President Ford
Served 1975 -

The unedited text of *Stone v. Graham* can be found on page 39, volume 449 of *United States Reports.*

STONE v. GRAHAM
November 17, 1980

PER CURIAM [by the entire Court]: A Kentucky statute
requires the posting of a copy of the Ten Commandments,
purchased with private contributions, on the wall of each
public classroom in the State. Petitioners [Stone et al.],
claiming that this statute violates the Establishment and
Free Exercise Clauses of the First Amendment, sought an
injunction [court order stopping an action] against its enforcement. The state trial court upheld the statute, finding that its "avowed purpose" was "secular and not religious," and that the statute would "neither advance nor inhibit any religion or religious group" nor involve the State
excessively in religious matters. The Supreme Court of
the Commonwealth of Kentucky affirmed [upheld]. . . .
We reverse.

This Court has announced [in *Lemon v. Kurtzman*] a
three-part test for determining whether a challenged state
statute is permissible under the Establishment Clause of
the United State Constitution:

> "First, the statute must have a secular legislative
> purpose; second, its principal or primary effect
> must be one that neither advances nor inhibits
> religion. . . ; finally the statute must not foster
> 'an excessive government entanglement with reli-
> gion.'"

If a statute violates any of these three principles, it must
be struck down under the Establishment Clause. We conclude that Kentucky's statute requiring the posting of the
Ten Commandments in public school rooms has no secular
legislative purpose, and is therefore unconstitutional.

The Commonwealth insists that the statute in question serves a secular legislative purpose, observing that the legislature required the following notation in small print at the bottom of each display of the Ten Commandments: "The secular application of the Ten Commandments is clearly seen in its adoption as the fundamental legal code of Western Civilization and the Common Law of the United States."

The trial court found the "avowed" purpose of the statute to be secular, even as it labeled the statutory declaration "self-serving." Under this Court's rulings, however, such an "avowed" secular purpose is not sufficient to avoid conflict with the First Amendment. In *Abington School District v. Schempp*, this Court held unconstitutional the daily reading of Bible verses and the Lord's Prayer in the public schools, despite the school district's assertion of such secular purposes as "the promotion of moral values, the contradiction to the materialistic trends of our times, the perpetuation of our institutions and the teaching of literature."

The pre-eminent purpose for posting the Ten Commandments on schoolroom walls is plainly religious in nature. The Ten Commandments are undeniably a sacred text in the Jewish and Christian faiths, and no legislative recitation of a supposed secular purpose can blind us to that fact. The Commandments do not confine themselves to arguably secular matters, such as honoring one's parents, killing or murder, adultery, stealing, false witness, and covetousness. Rather, the first part of the Commandments concerns the religious duties of believers: worshipping the Lord God alone, avoiding idolatry, not using the Lord's name in vain, and observing the Sabbath Day.

This is not a case in which the Ten Commandments are integrated into the school curriculum, where the Bible may constitutionally be used in an appropriate study of history, civilization, ethics, comparative religion, or the like. Posting of religious texts on the wall serves no such educational function. If the posted copies of the Ten Commandments are to have any effect at all, it will be to induce the schoolchildren to read, meditate upon, perhaps to venerate and obey, the Commandments. However desirable this might be as a matter of private devotion, it is not a permissible state objective under the Establishment Clause.

It does not matter that the posted copies of the Ten Commandments are financed by voluntary private contributions, for the mere posting of the copies under the auspices of the legislature provides the "official support of the State . . . Government" that the Establishment Clause prohibits. Nor is it significant that the Bible verses involved in this case are merely posted on the wall, rather than read aloud . . . , for "it is no defense to urge that the religious practices here may be relatively minor encroachments on the First Amendment." We conclude that [Kentucky's Ten Commandments Act] violates the first part of the *Lemon* test, and thus the Establishment Clause of the Constitution.

. . . . [T]he judgment [of the court] below is reversed.

It is so ordered.

The Creche Case
Lynch v. Donnelly

*For to you is born this day in the city of David a Savior,
who is Christ the Lord.*
- The Gospel According To St. Luke

A creche, depicting the reenactment of the Christian Nativity Scene, had been placed every year, for forty years,
in the downtown shopping district of Pawtucket, Rhode
Island, as part of an annual city-funded Christmas display.

In 1983 Pawtucket residents, including Daniel Donnelly,
in affiliation with the local chapter of the American Civil
Liberties Union (the ACLU), brought suit in U.S. District
Court against Pawtucket City officials, including Mayor
Dennis Lynch, challenging the inclusion of the creche in
its annual Christmas display as a violation of the First
Amendment's Establishment Clause.

Mayor Donnelly argued that, notwithstanding the religious significance of the creche, it was only a small part
of a larger secular Christmastime display and not, as argued by Donnelly, a violation of the separation of Church
and State. The District Court, rejecting this secular creche
argument, found that the inclusion of a symbol at the
heart of the Christian faith in a publicly-funded and sanc-
tioned display violated the Constitution's Establishment
Clause. Donnelly was granted a permanent injunction
against the City's future use of the creche in its annual
Christmas display. The City of Pawtucket appealed to the
U.S. Court of Appeals, which affirmed the District
Court's holding. Mayor Lynch appealed to the United
States Supreme Court.

Oral arguments were heard on October 4, 1983 and the
5-4 decision of the Court was announced on March 5,
1984 by Chief Justice Warren Burger.

THE LYNCH COURT

Chief Justice Warren Burger
Appointed Chief Justice by President Nixon
Served 1969 - 1986

Associate Justice William Brennan
Appointed by President Eisenhower
Served 1956 - 1990

Associate Justice Byron White
Appointed by President Kennedy
Served 1962 - 1993

Associate Justice Thurgood Marshall
Appointed by President Lyndon Johnson
Served 1967 - 1991

Associate Justice Harry Blackmun
Appointed by President Nixon
Served 1970 - 1994

Associate Justice Lewis Powell
Appointed by President Nixon
Served 1971 - 1987

Associate Justice William Rehnquist
Appointed by President Nixon
Served 1971 -

Associate Justice John Paul Stevens
Appointed by President Ford
Served 1975 -

Associate Justice Sandra Day O'Connor
Appointed by President Reagan
Served 1981 -

The unedited text of *Lynch v. Donnelly* can be found on page 668, volume 465 of *United States Reports.*

LYNCH v. DONNELLY
March 5, 1984

CHIEF JUSTICE BURGER: We granted certiorari [agreed to hear the case] to decide whether the Establishment Clause of the First Amendment prohibits a municipality from including a creche, or Nativity scene, in its annual Christmas display.

Each year, in cooperation with the downtown retail merchants' association, the city of Pawtucket, Rhode Island, erects a Christmas display as part of its observance of the Christmas holiday season. . . . The display is essentially like those to be found in hundreds of towns or cities across the Nation - often on public grounds - during the Christmas season. . . .

The creche, which has been included in the display for forty or more years, consists of the traditional figures, including the Infant Jesus, Mary and Joseph, angels, shepherds, kings, and animals. . . .

Respondents, Pawtucket residents and individual members of the Rhode Island affiliate of the American Civil Liberties Union, . . . brought this action in the United States District Court for Rhode Island, challenging the city's inclusion of the creche in the annual display. The District Court held that the city's inclusion of the creche in the display violates the Establishment Clause, which is binding on the states through the Fourteenth Amendment. The District Court found that, by including the creche in the Christmas display, the city has "tried to endorse and promulgate religious beliefs," and that "erection of the creche has the real and substantial effect of affiliating the City with the Christian beliefs that the creche represents."

This "appearance of official sponsorship," it believed, "confers more than a remote and incidental benefit on Christianity." . . . The city was permanently enjoined [prohibited] from including the creche in the display.

A divided panel of the Court of Appeals for the First Circuit affirmed [upheld]. We granted certiorari, and we reverse.

This Court has explained that the purpose of the Establishment and Free Exercise Clauses of the First Amendment is

"to prevent, as far as possible, the intrusion of either [the church or the state] into the precincts of the other."

At the same time, however, the Court has recognized that

"total separation is not possible in an absolute sense. Some relationship between government and religious organizations is inevitable."

In every Establishment Clause case, we must reconcile the inescapable tension between the objective of preventing unnecessary intrusion of either the church or the state upon the other, and the reality that, as the Court has so often noted, total separation of the two is not possible.

The Court has sometimes described the Religion Clauses as erecting a "wall" between church and state. The concept of a "wall" of separation is a useful figure of speech probably deriving from views of Thomas Jefferson. The metaphor has served as a reminder that the Establishment Clause forbids an established church or anything approaching it. But the metaphor itself is not a wholly accurate description of the practical aspects of the relationship that in fact exists between church and state.

. . . . The Court's interpretation of the Establishment Clause has comported with what history reveals was the contemporaneous understanding of its guarantees. A significant example of the contemporaneous understanding of that Clause is found in the events of the first week of the First Session of the First Congress in 1789. In the very week that Congress approved the Establishment Clause as part of the Bill of Rights for submission to the states, it enacted legislation providing for paid Chaplains for the House and Senate. . . .

The interpretation of the Establishment Clause by Congress in 1789 takes on special significance in light of the Court's emphasis that the First Congress

> "was a Congress whose constitutional decisions have always been regarded, as they should be regarded, as of the greatest weight in the interpretation of that fundamental instrument."

It is clear that neither the seventeen draftsmen of the Constitution who were Members of the First Congress, nor the Congress of 1789, saw any establishment problem in the employment of congressional Chaplains to offer daily prayers in the Congress, a practice that has continued for nearly two centuries. It would be difficult to identify a more striking example of the accommodation of religious belief intended by the Framers.

There is an unbroken history of official acknowledgment by all three branches of government of the role of religion in American life from at least 1789. Seldom in our opinions was this more affirmatively expressed than in Justice Douglas' opinion for the Court validating a program allowing release of public school students from classes to attend off-campus religious exercises. Rejecting a claim that the program violated the Establishment Clause, the Court asserted pointedly:

> "We are a religious people whose institutions presuppose a Supreme Being."

Our history is replete with official references to the value and invocation of Divine guidance in deliberations and pronouncements of the Founding Fathers and contemporary leaders. Beginning in the early colonial period long before Independence, a day of Thanksgiving was celebrated as a religious holiday to give thanks for the bounties of Nature as gifts from God. President Washington and his successors proclaimed Thanksgiving, with all its religious overtones, a day of national celebration and Congress made it a National Holiday more than a century ago. That holiday has not lost its theme of expressing thanks for Divine aid any more than has Christmas lost its religious significance.

. . . . Other examples of reference to our religious heritage are found in the statutorily prescribed national motto "In God We Trust," which Congress and the President mandated for our currency, and in the language "One nation under God," as part of the Pledge of Allegiance to the American flag. That pledge is recited by many thousands of public school children - and adults - every year.

. . . . This history may help explain why the Court consistently has declined to take a rigid, absolutist view of the

Establishment Clause. We have refused "to construe [interpret] the Religion Clauses with a literalness that would undermine the ultimate constitutional objective *as illuminated by history.*" In our modern, complex society, whose traditions and constitutional underpinnings rest on and encourage diversity and pluralism in all areas, an absolutist approach in applying the Establishment Clause is simplistic and has been uniformly rejected by the Court.

Rather than mechanically invalidating all governmental conduct or statutes that confer benefits or give special recognition to religion in general or to one faith - as an absolutist approach would dictate - the Court has scrutinized challenged legislation or official conduct to determine whether, in reality, it establishes a religion or religious faith, or tends to do so. Joseph Story wrote a century and a half ago:

> "The real object of the [First] Amendment was . . . to prevent any national ecclesiastical establishment, which should give to an hierarchy the exclusive patronage of the national government."

. . . . The narrow question is whether there is a secular purpose for Pawtucket's display of the creche. The display is sponsored by the city to celebrate the Holiday and to depict the origins of that Holiday. These are legitimate secular purposes. The District Court's inference, drawn from the religious nature of the creche, that the city has no secular purpose was, on this record, clearly erroneous.

. . . . We are satisfied that the city has a secular purpose for including the creche, that the city has not impermissibly advanced religion, and that including the creche does not create excessive entanglement between religion and government.

. . . . It would be ironic . . . if the inclusion of a single symbol of a particular historic religious event, as part of a celebration acknowledged in the Western World for twenty centuries, and in this country by the people, by the Executive Branch, by the Congress, and the courts for two centuries, would so "taint" the city's exhibit as to render it violative of the Establishment Clause. To forbid the use of this one passive symbol - the creche - at the very time people are taking note of the season with Christmas hymns and carols in public schools and other public places, and while the Congress and legislatures open sessions with prayers by paid chaplains, would be a stilted overreaction contrary to our history and to our holdings. If the presence of the creche in this display violates the Establishment Clause, a host of other forms of taking official note of Christmas, and of our religious heritage, are equally offensive to the Constitution.

The Court has acknowledged that the "fears and political problems" that gave rise to the Religion Clauses in the eighteenth century are of far less concern today. We are unable to perceive the Archbishop of Canterbury, the Bishop of Rome, or other powerful religious leaders behind every public acknowledgment of the religious heritage long officially recognized by the three constitutional branches of government. Any notion that these symbols pose a real danger of establishment of a state church is farfetched indeed.

. . . . We hold that, notwithstanding the religious significance of the creche, the city of Pawtucket has not violated the Establishment Clause of the First Amendment. Accordingly, the judgment of the Court of Appeals is reversed.

It is so ordered.

Islamic Prayers In Prison
O'Lone v. Shabazz

Woe be unto those who pray, and who are negligent at their prayer: who play the hypocrites, and deny necessaries to the needy.   **-The Koran**

Ahmad Uthman Shabazz, a member of the Islamic Faith, was incarcerated in New Jersey's Leesburg State Prison. Every Friday afternoon, as commanded by the Muslim Holy Book, The Koran, Shabazz and his fellow Muslim inmates participated in Jumu'ah, a weekly prayer service led by the prison's Imam in the main building.

To ease prison overcrowding the New Jersey Department of Corrections put into effect, in March 1983, a new policy which required selected inmates to be assigned to outside work details and away from the main building all day. This "Outside Work" policy prevented many Muslim inmates, including Shabazz, from attending Friday afternoon's Jumu'ah prayer services.

Ahmad Uthman Shabazz and other members of the Islamic Faith sued Edward O'Lone, Warden of Leesburg Prison, in U.S. District Court, claiming that the New Jersey Department of Correction's "Outside Work" policy, which he was charged with implementing, infringed upon their First Amendment Free Exercise rights. The District Court found for O'Lone, stating no constitutional violation of Shabazz's free exercise rights had occurred. Shabazz appealed to the U.S. Court of Appeals, which found O'Lone's implementation of the "Outside Work" policy had infringed upon Shabazz's free exercise rights. Warden O'Lone appealed to the United States Supreme Court.

Oral arguments were heard on March 24, 1987 and the 5-4 decision of the Court was announced on June 9, 1987 by Chief Justice William Rehnquist.

THE SHABAZZ COURT

Chief Justice William Rehnquist
Appointed Chief Justice by President Reagan
Appointed Associate Justice by President Nixon
Served 1971 -

Associate Justice William Brennan
Appointed by President Eisenhower
Served 1956 - 1990

Associate Justice Byron White
Appointed by President Kennedy
Served 1962 - 1993

Associate Justice Thurgood Marshall
Appointed by President Lyndon Johnson
Served 1967 - 1991

Associate Justice Harry Blackmun
Appointed by President Nixon
Served 1970 - 1994

Associate Justice Lewis Powell
Appointed by President Nixon
Served 1971 - 1987

Associate Justice John Paul Stevens
Appointed by President Ford
Served 1975 -

Associate Justice Sandra Day O'Connor
Appointed by President Reagan
Served 1981 -

Associate Justice Antonin Scalia
Appointed by President Reagan
Served 1986 -

The unedited text of *O'Lone v. Shabazz* can be found on page 342, volume 482 of *United States Reports.*

O'LONE v. SHABAZZ
June 9, 1987

CHIEF JUSTICE REHNQUIST: This case requires us to consider once again the standard of review for prison regulations claimed to inhibit the exercise of constitutional rights. Respondents, members of the Islamic faith, were prisoners in New Jersey's Leesburg State Prison. They challenged policies adopted by prison officials which resulted in their inability to attend Jumu'ah, a weekly Muslim congregational service regularly held in the main prison building and in a separate facility known as "the Farm." Jumu'ah is commanded by the Koran and must be held every Friday after the sun reaches its zenith and before the Asr, or afternoon prayer. There is no question that respondents' sincerely held religious beliefs compelled attendance at Jumu'ah. We hold that the prison regulations here challenged did not violate respondents' rights under the Free Exercise Clause of the First Amendment to the United States Constitution.

. . . . Because of serious overcrowding in the [prison's] main building, [the New Jersey Department of Corrections] . . . mandated that [selected] inmates ordinarily be assigned jobs outside the main building. . . . In the initial stages of outside work details for . . . minimum [security] prisoners, officials apparently allowed some Muslim inmates to work inside the main building on Fridays so that they could attend Jumu'ah. . . .

Significant problems arose with those inmates assigned to outside work details. . . .

In response to these [problems], Leesburg officials took steps to ensure that those assigned to outside details remained there for the whole day. . . . [P]rison officials in March 1984 issued a policy memorandum which prohibited inmates assigned to outside work details from returning to the prison during the day except in the case of emergency.

The prohibition of returns prevented Muslims assigned to outside work details from attending Jumu'ah. Respondents filed suit . . . , alleging that the prison policies unconstitutionally denied them their Free Exercise rights under the First Amendment, as applied to the States through the Fourteenth Amendment. The District Court . . . concluded that no constitutional violation had occurred. . . .

The Court of Appeals . . . decided that . . . the District Court was not sufficiently protective of prisoners' free exercise rights. . . .

We granted certiorari [agreed to hear the case] to consider the important federal constitutional issues presented by the Court of Appeals' decision. . . .

Several general principles guide our consideration of the issues presented here. First, "convicted prisoners do not forfeit all constitutional protections by reason of their conviction and confinement in prison." Inmates clearly retain protections afforded by the First Amendment, including its directive that no law shall prohibit the free exercise of religion. Second, "[l]awful incarceration brings about the necessary withdrawal or limitation of many privileges and rights, a retraction justified by the considerations underlying our penal system." The limitations on the exercise of constitutional rights arise both from the fact of incarceration and from valid penological objectives - including deterrence of crime, rehabilitation of prisoners, and institutional security.

In considering the appropriate balance of these factors, we have often said that evaluation of penological objectives is committed to the considered judgment of prison administrators, "who are actually charged with and trained in the running of the particular institution under examination." To ensure that courts afford appropriate deference to prison officials, we have determined that prison regulations alleged to infringe constitutional rights are judged under a "reasonableness" test less restrictive than that ordinarily applied to alleged infringements of fundamental constitutional rights. We recently restated the proper standard [in *Turner*]: "[W]hen a prison regulation impinges on inmates' constitutional rights, the regulation is valid if it is reasonably related to legitimate penological interests." ...

We think the Court of Appeals decision in this case was wrong when it established a separate burden on prison officials to prove "that no reasonable method exists by which [prisoners'] religious rights can be accommodated without creating bona fide security problems." ...

Our decision in *Turner* also found it relevant that "alternative means of exercising the right ... remain open to prison inmates." There are, of course, no alternative means of attending Jumu'ah; respondents' religious beliefs insist that it occur at a particular time. But the very stringent requirements as to the time at which Jumu'ah may be held may make it extraordinarily difficult for prison officials to assure that every Muslim prisoner is able to attend that service. While we in no way minimize the central importance of Jumu'ah to respondents, we are unwilling to hold that prison officials are required by the Constitution to sacrifice legitimate penological objectives to that end. ... [W]e think it appropriate to see whether under these regulations respondents retain the ability to participate in other Muslim religious ceremonies. The record establishes that respondents are not deprived of all forms of religious exercise, but instead freely observe a number of their religious obligations. The right to congregate for prayer or discussion is "virtually unlimited except during working hours," and the state-provided imam has free access to the prison. Muslim prisoners are given different meals whenever pork is served in the prison cafeteria. Special arrangements are also made during the month-long observance of Ramadan, a period of fasting and prayer. During Ramadan, Muslim prisoners are awakened at 4 a.m. for an early breakfast, and receive dinner at 8:30 each evening. We think this ability on the part of respondents to participate in other religious observances of their faith supports the conclusion that the restrictions at issue here were reasonable.

Finally, the case for the validity of these regulations is strengthened by examination of the impact that accommodation of respondents' asserted right would have on other inmates, on prison personnel, and on allocation of prison resources generally. Respondents suggest several accommodations of their practices, including placing all Muslim inmates in one or two inside work details or providing weekend labor for Muslim inmates. As noted by the District Court, however, each of respondents' suggested accommodations would, in the judgment of prison officials, have adverse effects on the institution. ... These concerns of prison administrators provide adequate support for the conclusion that accommodations of respondents' request to attend Jumu'ah would have undesirable results in the institution. These difficulties also make clear that there are no "obvious, easy alternatives to the policy adopted by petitioners."

We take this opportunity to reaffirm our refusal, even where claims are made under the First Amendment, to "substitute our judgment on . . . difficult and sensitive matters of institutional administration," for the determinations of those charged with the formidable task of running a prison. Here the District Court decided that the regulations alleged to infringe constitutional rights were reasonably related to legitimate penological objectives. We agree with the District Court, and it necessarily follows that the regulations in question do not offend the Free Exercise Clause of the First Amendment to the United States Constitution. The judgment of the Court of Appeals is therefore reversed.

Distribution Of Religious Literature
LAX v. Jews For Jesus

The Central Terminal Area at Los Angeles International Airport is not open for First Amendment activities by any individual and/or entity.
-LAX's First Amendment Activities Ban

On July 13, 1983 the Board of Commissioners for Los Angeles International Airport (LAX) passed a Resolution banning all "First Amendment activities" at the Airport's Central Terminal Area. The Resolution plainly stated: "Los Angeles International Airport is not open for First Amendment activities by any individual and/or entity." The Resolution further directed the Los Angeles City Attorney to prosecute any person or group violating their First Amendment Activities Ban.

On July 6, 1984 Alan Howard Snyder, a Minister of the Gospel for the Jews for Jesus, while in the process of distributing free religious literature at LAX's Central Terminal, was informed by the Airport Police that he was in violation of the First Amendment Activities Ban and asked to leave. Snyder, under threat of arrest, complied.

The Jews for Jesus filed suit in U.S. District Court, challenging both the constitutionality of LAX's ban on religious expression and its selective enforcement against them. The District Court held that the Central Terminal Area was a public forum protected by the Constitution and struck down the First Amendment Activities Ban. The U.S. Court of Appeals upheld the District Court's decision. The Board of Airport Commissioners appealed for a reversal to the United States Supreme Court.

Oral arguments were heard on March 3, 1987 and the 9-0 decision of the Court was announced on June 15, 1987 by Associate Justice Sandra Day O'Connor.

THE JEWS FOR JESUS COURT

Chief Justice William Rehnquist
Appointed Chief Justice by President Reagan
Appointed Associate Justice by President Nixon
Served 1971 -

Associate Justice William Brennan
Appointed by President Eisenhower
Served 1956 - 1990

Associate Justice Byron White
Appointed by President Kennedy
Served 1962 - 1993

Associate Justice Thurgood Marshall
Appointed by President Lyndon Johnson
Served 1967 - 1991

Associate Justice Harry Blackmun
Appointed by President Nixon
Served 1970 - 1994

Associate Justice Lewis Powell
Appointed by President Nixon
Served 1971 - 1987

Associate Justice John Paul Stevens
Appointed by President Ford
Served 1975 -

Associate Justice Sandra Day O'Connor
Appointed by President Reagan
Served 1981 -

Associate Justice Antonin Scalia
Appointed by President Reagan
Served 1986 -

The unedited text of *LAX v. Jews For Jesus* can be found on page 569, volume 482 of *United States Reports.*

LAX v. JEWS FOR JESUS
June 15, 1987

JUSTICE O'CONNOR: The issue presented in this case is whether a resolution banning all "First Amendment activities" at Los Angeles International Airport (LAX) violates the First Amendment.

On July 13, 1983, the Board of Airport Commissioners adopted [a] Resolution, which provides in pertinent part:

> "NOW, THEREFORE, BE IT RESOLVED by the Board of Airport Commissioners that the Central Terminal Area at Los Angeles International Airport is not open for First Amendment activities by any individual and/or entity; . . . .

> "BE IT FURTHER RESOLVED that after the effective date of this Resolution, if any individual and/or entity seeks to engage in First Amendment activities within the Central Terminal Area at Los Angeles International Airport, said individual and/or entity shall be deemed to be acting in contravention of the stated policy of the Board of Airport Commissioners in reference to the uses permitted within the Central Terminal Area at Los Angeles International Airport; and

> "BE IT FURTHER RESOLVED that if any individual or entity engages in First Amendment activities within the Central Terminal Area at Los Angeles International Airport, the City Attorney of the City of Los Angeles is directed to institute appropriate litigation against such individual and/or entity to ensure compliance with this Poli-

cy statement of the Board of Airport Commissioners. . . ."

Respondent Jews for Jesus, Inc., is a nonprofit religious corporation. On July 6, 1984, Alan Howard Snyder, a minister of the Gospel for Jews for Jesus, was stopped by a Department of Airports peace officer while distributing free religious literature on a pedestrian walkway in the Central Terminal Area at LAX. The officer showed Snyder a copy of the resolution, explained that Snyder's activities violated the resolution, and requested that Snyder leave LAX. The officer warned Snyder that the city would take legal action against him if he refused to leave as requested. Snyder stopped distributing the leaflets and left the airport terminal.

Jews for Jesus and Snyder then filed this action in [U.S.] District Court . . . , challenging the constitutionality of the resolution under . . . the First Amendment to the United States Constitution because it bans all speech in a public forum. . . .

The District Court held that the Central Terminal Area was a traditional public forum under federal law, and that the resolution was facially unconstitutional under the United States Constitution. . . . The [U.S.] Court of Appeals . . . affirmed [upheld]. . . . [T]he Court of Appeals concluded that "an airport complex is a traditional public forum," and held that the resolution was unconstitutional on its face under the Federal Constitution. We granted certiorari [agreed to hear the case], and now affirm, but on different grounds.

.... [W]e conclude that the resolution is facially unconstitutional under the First Amendment overbreadth doctrine. ...

Under the First Amendment overbreadth doctrine, an individual whose own speech or conduct may be prohibited
is permitted to challenge a statute on its face "because it
also threatens others not before the court - those who desire to engage in legally protected expression but who
may refrain from doing so rather than risk prosecution or
undertake to have the law declared partially invalid." A
statute may be invalidated on its face, however, only if the
overbreadth is "substantial." The requirement that the
overbreadth be substantial arose from our recognition that
application of the overbreadth doctrine is, "manifestly,
strong medicine," and that "there must be a realistic danger that the statute itself will significantly compromise
recognized First Amendment protections of parties not
before the Court for it to be facially challenged on overbreadth grounds."

On its face, the resolution at issue in this case reaches the
universe of expressive activity, and, by prohibiting *all*
protected expression, purports to create a virtual "First
Amendment Free Zone" at LAX. The resolution does not
merely regulate expressive activity in the Central Terminal Area that might create problems such as congestion or
the disruption of the activities of those who use LAX. Instead, the resolution expansively states that LAX "is not
open for First Amendment activities by any individual
and/or entity," and that "any individual and/or entity
[who] seeks to engage in First Amendment activities within the Central Terminal Area . . . shall be deemed to be
acting in contravention of the stated policy of the Board
of Airport Commissioners." The resolution therefore does

not merely reach the activity of respondents at LAX; it prohibits even talking and reading, or the wearing of campaign buttons or symbolic clothing. Under such a sweeping ban, virtually every individual who enters LAX may be found to violate the resolution by engaging in some "First Amendment activit[y]." We think it obvious that such a ban cannot be justified even if LAX were a nonpublic forum because no conceivable governmental interest would justify such an absolute prohibition of speech.

. . . . The petitioners [LAX] suggest that the resolution is not substantially overbroad because it is intended to reach only expressive activity unrelated to airport-related purposes. Such a limiting construction, however, is of little assistance in substantially reducing the overbreadth of the resolution. Much nondisruptive speech - such as the wearing of a T-shirt or button that contains a political message - may not be "airport related," but is still protected speech even in a nonpublic forum. Moreover, the vagueness of this suggested construction itself presents serious constitutional difficulty. The line between airport-related speech and nonairport-related speech is, at best, murky. The petitioners, for example, suggest that an individual who reads a newspaper or converses with a neighbor at LAX is engaged in permitted "airport-related" activity because reading or conversing permits the traveling public to "pass the time." We presume, however, that petitioners would not so categorize the activities of a member of a religious or political organization who decides to "pass the time" by distributing leaflets to fellow travelers. In essence, the result of this vague limiting construction would be to give LAX officials alone the power to decide in the first instance whether a given activity is airport related. Such a law that "confers on police a virtually unrestrained power to arrest and charge persons with a violation" of the resolution is unconstitutional because "[t]he opportunity for abuse, especially where a statute has received a virtually open-ended interpretation, is self-evident."

We conclude that the resolution is substantially overbroad, and is not fairly subject to a limiting construction. Accordingly, we hold that the resolution violates the First Amendment. The judgment of the Court of Appeals is affirmed.

Prayers At Graduation
Lee v. Weisman

O God, we are grateful to You for having endowed us with the capacity for learning which we have celebrated on this joyous commencement.

- The Providence Graduation Prayer

On June 29, 1989 at the invitation of Robert E. Lee, Principal of the Nathan Bishop Middle School in Providence, Rhode Island, a local clergyman, Rabbi Leslie Gutterman, was asked to offer invocation and benediction prayers as part of the school's graduation ceremony. The prayers were to be structured in accordance with the National Conference of Christians and Jews' "Guidelines For Civic Occasions," which recommended that at nonsectarian civic ceremonies, such as public school graduations, prayers be composed with elements of inclusiveness and sensitivity.

Deborah Weisman, a fourteen-year-old graduating senior, objected to the inclusion of any prayer at the ceremonies. Four days before the graduation Deborah's father, Daniel, brought suit in Federal District Court to prohibit the prayers, claiming they violated the First Amendment's Establishment Clause. The District Court, citing a lack of adequate time to consider the matter, denied the Weismans' request and the prayers were said at the graduation.

The Weismans continued their suit against Principal Lee to prevent any future graduation prayers in Providence schools. This time the U.S. District Court held for the Weismans, finding that the prayers were an impermissible governmental endorsement of religion. Lee appealed to the U.S. Court of Appeals, which affirmed the decision. Lee then appealed to the United States Supreme Court.

Oral arguments were heard on November 6, 1991 and the 5-4 decision of the Court was announced on June 24, 1992 by Associate Justice Anthony Kennedy.

THE WEISMAN COURT

Chief Justice William Rehnquist
Appointed Chief Justice by President Reagan
Appointed Associate Justice by President Nixon
Served 1971 -

Associate Justice Byron White
Appointed by President Kennedy
Served 1962 - 1993

Associate Justice Harry Blackmun
Appointed by President Nixon
Served 1970 - 1994

Associate Justice John Paul Stevens
Appointed by President Ford
Served 1975 -

Associate Justice Sandra Day O'Connor
Appointed by President Reagan
Served 1981 -

Associate Justice Antonin Scalia
Appointed by President Reagan
Served 1986 -

Associate Justice Anthony Kennedy
Appointed by President Reagan
Served 1988 -

Associate Justice David Souter
Appointed by President Bush
Served 1990 -

Associate Justice Clarence Thomas
Appointed by President Bush
Served 1991 -

The unedited text of *Lee v. Weisman* can be found on page 577, volume 512 of *United States Reports.*

LEE v. WEISMAN
June 24, 1992

JUSTICE KENNEDY: School principals in the public school system of the city of Providence, Rhode Island, are permitted to invite members of the clergy to offer invocation and benediction prayers as part of the formal graduation ceremonies for middle schools and for high schools. The question before us is whether including clerical members who offer prayers as part of the official school graduation ceremony is consistent with the Religion Clauses of the First Amendment, provisions the Fourteenth Amendment makes applicable with full force to the States and their school districts.

Deborah Weisman graduated from Nathan Bishop Middle School, a public school in Providence, at a formal ceremony in June 1989. She was about fourteen years old. For many years it has been the policy of the Providence School Committee and the Superintendent of Schools to permit principals to invite members of the clergy to give invocations and benedictions at middle school and high school graduations. Many, but not all, of the principals elected to include prayers as part of the graduation ceremonies. Acting for himself and his daughter, Deborah's father, Daniel Weisman, objected to any prayers at Deborah's middle school graduation, but to no avail. The school principal, petitioner Robert E. Lee, invited a rabbi to deliver prayers at the graduation exercises for Deborah's class. Rabbi Leslie Gutterman, of the Temple Beth El in Providence, accepted.

. . . . Rabbi Gutterman's prayers were as follows:

"INVOCATION

"God of the Free, Hope of the Brave:

"For the legacy of America where diversity is celebrated and the rights of minorities are protected, we thank You. May these young men and women grow up to enrich it.

"For the liberty of America, we thank You. May these new graduates grow up to guard it.

"For the political process of America in which all its citizens may participate, for its court system where all may seek justice we thank You. May those we honor this morning always turn to it in trust.

"For the destiny of America we thank You. May the graduates of Nathan Bishop Middle School so live that they might help to share it.

"May our aspirations for our country and for these young people, who are our hope for the future, be richly fulfilled.

AMEN"

"BENEDICTION

"O God, we are grateful to You for having endowed us with the capacity for learning which we have celebrated on this joyous commencement.

"Happy families give thanks for seeing their children achieve an important milestone. Send Your blessings upon the teachers and administrators who helped prepare them.

"The graduates now need strength and guidance for the future, help them to understand that we are not complete with academic knowledge alone. We must each strive to fulfill what You require of us all: To do justly, to love mercy, to walk humbly.

"We give thanks to You, Lord, for keeping us alive, sustaining us and allowing us to reach this special, happy occasion.

AMEN"

.... The school board (and the United States, which supports it as *amicus curiae* [friend of the Court]) argued that these short prayers and others like them at graduation exercises are of profound meaning to many students and parents throughout this country who consider that due respect and acknowledgment for divine guidance and for the deepest spiritual aspirations of our people ought to be expressed at an event as important in life as a graduation. We assume this to be so in addressing the difficult case now before us, for the significance of the prayers lies also at the heart of Daniel and Deborah Weisman's case.

Deborah's graduation was held on the premises of Nathan Bishop Middle School on June 29, 1989. Four days before the ceremony, Daniel Weisman . . . sought a temporary restraining order in the United States District Court for the District of Rhode Island to prohibit school officials from including an invocation or benediction in the graduation ceremony. The court denied the motion for lack of adequate time to consider it. Deborah and her family attended the graduation, where the prayers were recited. In July 1989, Daniel Weisman filed an amended complaint seeking a permanent injunction [court order stopping an action] barring petitioners, various officials of the Providence public schools, from inviting the clergy to deliver invocations and benedictions at future graduations. ... Deborah Weisman is enrolled as a student at Classical High School in Providence and from the record it appears likely, if not certain, that an invocation and benediction will be conducted at her high school graduation.

.... The District Court held that petitioners' practice of including invocations and benedictions in public school graduations violated the Establishment Clause of the First Amendment, and it enjoined [prohibited] petitioners from continuing the practice. ...

On appeal, the United States Court of Appeals for the First Circuit affirmed [upheld]. ... We granted certiorari [agreed to hear the case], and now affirm.

These dominant facts mark and control the confines of our decision: State officials direct the performance of a formal religious exercise at promotional and graduation ceremonies for secondary schools. Even for those students who object to the religious exercise, their attendance and participation in the state-sponsored religious activity are in a fair and real sense obligatory, though the school district does not require attendance as a condition for receipt of the diploma.

.... The government involvement with religious activity in this case is pervasive, to the point of creating a state-sponsored and state-directed religious exercise in a public school. Conducting this formal religious observance conflicts with settled rules pertaining to prayer exercises for students, and that suffices to determine the question before us.

The principle that government may accommodate the free exercise of religion does not supersede the fundamental limitations imposed by the Establishment Clause. It is beyond dispute that, at a minimum, the Constitution guarantees that government may not coerce anyone to support or participate in religion or its exercise, or otherwise act in a way which "establishes a [state] religion or religious faith, or tends to do so." The State's involvement in the school prayers challenged today violates these central principles.

That involvement is as troubling as it is undenied. A school official, the principal, decided that an invocation and a benediction should be given; this is a choice attributable to the State, and from a constitutional perspective it is as if a state statute decreed that the prayers must occur. The principal chose the religious participant, here a rabbi, and that choice is also attributable to the State....

The State's role did not end with the decision to include a prayer and with the choice of clergyman. Principal Lee provided Rabbi Gutterman with a copy of the "Guidelines for Civic Occasions," and advised him that his prayers should be nonsectarian. Through these means the principal directed and controlled the content of the prayers.... It is a cornerstone principle of our Establishment Clause jurisprudence that "it is no part of the business of government to compose official prayers for any group of the

American people to recite as a part of a religious program carried on by government," and that is what the school officials attempted to do.

. . . . The First Amendment's Religion Clauses mean that religious beliefs and religious expression are too precious to be either proscribed or prescribed by the State. The design of the Constitution is that preservation and transmission of religious beliefs and worship is a responsibility and a choice committed to the private sphere, which itself is promised freedom to pursue that mission. It must not be forgotten then, that while concern must be given to define the protection granted to an objector or a dissenting nonbeliever, these same Clauses exist to protect religion from government interference. . . .

These concerns have particular application in the case of school officials, whose effort to monitor prayer will be perceived by the students as inducing a participation they might otherwise reject. Though the efforts of the school officials in this case to find common ground appear to have been a good-faith attempt to recognize the common aspects of religions and not the divisive ones, our precedents do not permit school officials to assist in composing prayers as an incident to a formal exercise for their students. . . .

The degree of school involvement here made it clear that the graduation prayers bore the imprint of the State and thus put school-age children who objected in an untenable position. . . .

The injury caused by the government's action, and the reason why Daniel and Deborah Weisman object to it, is that the State, in a school setting, in effect required participation in a religious exercise. It is, we concede, a brief exercise during which the individual can concentrate on joining its message, meditate on her own religion, or let her mind wander. But the embarrassment and the intrusion of the religious exercise cannot be refuted by arguing that these prayers, and similar ones to be said in the future, are of a *de minimis* [insignificant] character. To do so would be an affront to the rabbi who offered them and to all those for whom the prayers were an essential and profound recognition of divine authority. And for the same reason, we think that the intrusion is greater than the two minutes or so of time consumed for prayers like these. Assuming, as we must, that the prayers were offensive to the student and the parent who now object, the intrusion was both real and, in the context of a secondary school, a violation of the objectors' rights. That the intrusion was in the course of promulgating religion that sought to be civic or nonsectarian rather than pertaining to one sect does not lessen the offense or isolation to the objectors. At best it narrows their number, at worst increases their sense of isolation and affront.

. . . . The sole question presented is whether a religious exercise may be conducted at a graduation ceremony in circumstances where, as we have found, young graduates who object are induced to conform. No holding by this Court suggests that a school can persuade or compel a student to participate in a religious exercise. That is being done here, and it is forbidden by the Establishment Clause of the First Amendment.

For the reasons we have stated, the judgment of the Court of Appeals is affirmed.

Ritual Animal Sacrifice
Santeria Church v. Hialeah

It shall be unlawful for any person, persons, corporations, or associations to sacrifice any animal within the corporate limits of the City of Hialeah.
- Hialeah's Anti-Animal Sacrifice Ordinance

The Santeria religion, called "the way of the saints," is a fusion of traditional African and Roman Catholic worship created in nineteenth century Cuba by kidnapped African slaves. Santeria uses as one of its principal forms of worship the practice of animal sacrifice.

In early 1987 Ernesto Pichardo, *Italero* (High Priest) of the Santeria Congregation of the Church of the Lukumi Babalu Aye, a not-for-profit Florida corporation, announced plans to establish a Santeria house of worship in the City of Hialeah to serve a portion of the estimated 50,000 Santeria followers living in South Florida.

In response Hialeah, concerned that "certain religions may engage in practices inconsistent with public morals," enacted several Anti-Animal Sacrifice Ordinances.

Italero Pichardo and the Santeria Church sued the City of Hialeah in U.S. District Court, asserting these Anti-Animal Sacrifice Ordinances were a violation of their right to worship free of government interference under the First Amendment's Free Exercise Clause. The Federal District Court found the Hialeah Ordinances constitutional. Pichardo and the Church appealed to the U.S. Court of Appeals for a reversal. The Federal Appeals Court affirmed the District Court's decision. *Italero* Pichardo and the Santeria Church appealed to the U.S. Supreme Court.

Oral arguments were heard on November 4, 1992 and the 9-0 decision of the Court was announced on June 11, 1993 by Justice Anthony Kennedy.

THE SANTERIA CHURCH COURT

Chief Justice William Rehnquist
Appointed Chief Justice by President Reagan
Appointed Associate Justice by President Nixon
Served 1971 -

Associate Justice Byron White
Appointed by President Kennedy
Served 1962 -

Associate Justice Harry Blackmun
Appointed by President Nixon
Served 1970 - 1994

Associate Justice John Paul Stevens
Appointed by President Ford
Served 1975 -

Associate Justice Sandra Day O'Connor
Appointed by President Reagan
Served 1981 -

Associate Justice Antonin Scalia
Appointed by President Reagan
Served 1986 -

Associate Justice Anthony Kennedy
Appointed by President Reagan
Served 1988 -

Associate Justice David Souter
Appointed by President Bush
Served 1990 -

Associate Justice Clarence Thomas
Appointed by President Bush
Served 1991 -

The unedited text of *Santeria Church v. Hialeah* can be found in volume 508 of *United States Reports.*

SANTERIA CHURCH v. HIALEAH
June 11, 1993

JUSTICE KENNEDY: The principle that government may not enact laws that suppress religious belief or practice is so well understood that few violations are recorded in our opinions. Concerned that this fundamental non-persecution principle of the First Amendment was implicated here, however, we granted certiorari [agreed to hear the case].

. . . . This case involves practices of the Santeria religion, which originated in the nineteenth century. When hundreds of thousands of members of the Yoruba people were brought as slaves from eastern Africa to Cuba, their traditional African religion absorbed significant elements of Roman Catholicism. The resulting syncretion, or fusion, is Santeria, "the way of the saints." . . .

The Santeria faith teaches that every individual has a destiny from God, a destiny fulfilled with the aid and energy of the *orishas* [spirits]. The basis of the Santeria religion is the nurture of a personal relation with the *orishas,* and one of the principal forms of devotion is an animal sacrifice. . . .

[The p]etitioner [is the] Church of the Lukumi Babalu Aye. . . . The Church and its congregants practice the Santeria religion. The president of the Church is petitioner Ernesto Pichardo, who is also the Church's priest and holds the religious title of *Italero,* the second highest in the Santeria faith. In April 1987, the Church leased land in the city of Hialeah, Florida, and announced plans to establish a house of worship. . . .

The prospect of a Santeria church in their midst was distressing to many members of the Hialeah community. . . .

In September 1987, the [Hialeah] city council adopted three substantive ordinances [prohibiting] religious animal sacrifice. . . .

Following enactment of these ordinances, the Church and Pichardo filed this action [against the City of Hialeah] . . . in the United States District Court . . . [alleging] violations of [the Church's] rights under . . . the Free Exercise Clause. . . .

[T]he District Court ruled for the city, finding no violation of [the Church's] rights under the Free Exercise Clause. . . .

The Court of Appeals . . . affirmed [upheld, stating that] the ordinances were consistent with the Constitution.

The Free Exercise Clause of the First Amendment, which has been applied to the States through the Fourteenth Amendment provides that "Congress shall make no law respecting an establishment of religion, or *prohibiting the free exercise thereof.* . . ." The city does not argue that Santeria is not a "religion" within the meaning of the First Amendment. Nor could it. Although the practice of animal sacrifice may seem abhorrent to some, "religious beliefs need not be acceptable, logical, consistent, or comprehensible to others in order to merit First Amendment protection." . . . Neither the city nor the [lower courts], moreover, have questioned the sincerity of [the church's] professed desire to conduct animal sacrifices for religious reasons. We must consider [their] First Amendment claim.

In addressing the constitutional protection for free exercise of religion, our cases establish the general proposition that a law that is neutral and of general applicability need not be justified by a compelling governmental interest even if the law has the incidental effect of burdening a particular religious practice. Neutrality and general applicability are interrelated, and, as becomes apparent in this case, failure to satisfy one requirement is a likely indication that the other has not been satisfied. A law failing to satisfy these requirements must be justified by a compelling governmental interest and must be narrowly tailored to advance that interest. These ordinances fail to satisfy [these] requirements. We begin by discussing neutrality.

. . . . The record in this case compels the conclusion that suppression of the central element of the Santeria worship service was the object of the ordinances. . . .

That the ordinances were enacted "'because of,' not merely 'in spite of,'" their suppression of Santeria religious practice is revealed by the events preceding enactment of the ordinances. Although [Hialeah] claimed that it had experienced significant problems resulting from the sacrifice of animals within the city before the announced opening of the Church, the city council made no attempt to address the supposed problem [until] just weeks after the Church announced plans to open. . . .

This history discloses the object of the ordinances to target animal sacrifice by Santeria worshippers because of its religious motivation.

In sum, the neutrality inquiry leads to one conclusion: The ordinances had as their object the suppression of religion.

The pattern we have recited discloses animosity to Santeria adherents and their religious practices. . . . These ordinances are not neutral, and the court below committed clear error in failing to reach this conclusion.

We turn next to a second requirement of the Free Exercise Clause, the rule that laws burdening religious practice must be of general applicability. All laws are selective to some extent, but categories of selection are of paramount concern when a law has the incidental effect of burdening religious practice. The Free Exercise Clause "protect[s] religious observers against unequal treatment," and inequality results when a legislature decides that the governmental interests it seeks to advance are worthy of being pursued only against conduct with a religious motivation.

The principle that government, in pursuit of legitimate interests, cannot in a selective manner impose burdens only on conduct motivated by religious belief is essential to the protection of the rights guaranteed by the Free Exercise Clause. . . . In this case we need not define with precision the standard used to evaluate whether a prohibition is of general application, for these ordinances fall well below the minimum standard necessary to protect First Amendment rights.

. . . . We conclude, in sum, that each of Hialeah's ordinances pursues the city's governmental interests only against conduct motivated by religious belief. The ordinances "ha[ve] every appearance of a prohibition that society is prepared to impose upon [Santeria worshippers] but not upon itself."

.... The Free Exercise Clause commits government itself to religious tolerance, and upon even slight suspicion that proposals for state intervention stem from animosity to religion or distrust of its practices, all officials must pause to remember their own high duty to the Constitution and to the rights it secures. Those in office must be resolute in resisting importunate demands and must ensure that the sole reasons for imposing the burdens of law and regulation are secular. Legislators may not devise mechanisms, overt or disguised, designed to persecute or oppress a religion or its practices. The laws here in question were enacted contrary to these constitutional principles, and they are void.

Reversed.

The Jewish School District
Kiryas Joel Village Schools v. Grumet

The Village of Kiryas Joel in the town of Monroe is hereby constituted as a separate school district and shall have and enjoy all the powers and duties of a school district.
-New York's Kiryas Joel School District Act

The Satmar Hasidim, an ultra-orthodox Jewish sect, purchased 320 acres in Orange County, New York, within the Town of Monroe. In 1977 they incorporated this area to form the Village of Kiryas Joel, an exclusive Satmar-only religious enclave, which grew to a population of 8,500.

Kiryas Joel had two parochial schools. Neither offered, as required by law, special services to physically, mentally, or emotionally disabled children. The Monroe-Woodbury Public School District, into which Kiryas Joel fell, offered these special disability services but was barred by law from providing these services outside their own public facilities. The parents of Kiryas Joel's disabled children were told to either send their children to the public schools, pay for the services themselves, or do without. In 1989 New York State, to solve this problem, enacted the "Kiryas Joel Village Act" which created a Kiryas Joel *Public* School District. The Law allowed public funding of Kiryas Joel's parochial school-based programs for disabled children.

Louis Grumet, an officer of the New York State School Boards Association brought suit in the New York Courts, claiming that the Kiryas Joel School District Act violated the First Amendment's Establishment Clause. Three New York Courts agreed. The Kiryas Joel Village School District appealed to the United States Supreme Court.

Oral arguments were heard on March 30, 1994 and the 6-3 decision of the Court was announced on June 27, 1994 by Associate Justice David Souter.

THE KIRYAS JOEL COURT

Chief Justice William Rehnquist
Appointed Chief Justice by President Reagan
Appointed Associate Justice by President Nixon
Served 1971 -

Associate Justice Harry Blackmun
Appointed by President Nixon
Served 1970 - 1994

Associate Justice John Paul Stevens
Appointed by President Ford
Served 1975 -

Associate Justice Sandra Day O'Connor
Appointed by President Reagan
Served 1981 -

Associate Justice Antonin Scalia
Appointed by President Reagan
Served 1986 -

Associate Justice Anthony Kennedy
Appointed by President Reagan
Served 1988 -

Associate Justice David Souter
Appointed by President Bush
Served 1990 -

Associate Justice Clarence Thomas
Appointed by President Bush
Served 1991 -

Associate Justice Ruth Bader Ginsburg
Appointed by President Clinton
Served 1993 -

The unedited text of *Kiryas Joel Village Schools v. Grumet* can be found in volume 512 of *United States Reports.*

KIRYAS JOEL SCHOOL DISTRICT
v. GRUMET
June 27, 1994

JUSTICE SOUTER: The Village of Kiryas Joel in Orange County, New York, is a religious enclave of Satmar Hasidim, practitioners of a strict form of Judaism. The village fell within the Monroe-Woodbury Central School District until a special state statute passed in 1989 carved out a separate district, following village lines, to serve this distinctive population. The question is whether the [Kiryas Joel School District law] creating the separate school district violates the Establishment Clause of the First Amendment, binding on the States through the Fourteenth Amendment. Because this unusual act is tantamount to an allocation of political power on a religious criterion and neither presupposes nor requires governmental impartiality toward religion, we hold that it violates the prohibition against establishment.

The Satmar Hasidic sect takes its name from the town near the Hungarian and Romanian border where, in the early years of this century, Grand Rebbe Joel Teitelbaum molded the group into a distinct community. After World War II and the destruction of much of European Jewry, the Grand Rebbe and most of his surviving followers moved to the Williamsburg section of Brooklyn, New York. Then, twenty years ago, the Satmars purchased an approved but undeveloped subdivision in the town of Monroe and began assembling the community that has since become the Village of Kiryas Joel. When a zoning dispute arose in the course of settlement, the Satmars presented the Town Board of Monroe with a petition to form a new village within the town, a right that New York's

Village Law gives almost any group of residents who satisfy certain procedural niceties. Neighbors who did not wish to secede with the Satmars objected strenuously, and after arduous negotiations the proposed boundaries of the Village of Kiryas Joel were drawn to include just the 320 acres owned and inhabited entirely by Satmars. . . .

The residents of Kiryas Joel are vigorously religious people who make few concessions to the modern world and go to great lengths to avoid assimilation into it. They interpret the Torah strictly; segregate the sexes outside the home; speak Yiddish as their primary language; eschew television, radio, and English-language publications; and dress in distinctive ways that include headcoverings and special garments for boys and modest dresses for girls. Children are educated in private religious schools, most boys at the United Talmudic Academy where they receive a thorough grounding in the Torah and limited exposure to secular subjects, and most girls at Bais Rochel, an affiliated school with a curriculum designed to prepare girls for their roles as wives and mothers.

These schools do not, however, offer any distinctive services to handicapped children, who are entitled under state and federal law to special education services even when enrolled in private schools. . . . Children from Kiryas Joel who needed special education (including the deaf, the mentally retarded, and others suffering from a range of physical, mental, or emotional disorders) were then forced to attend public schools outside the village, which their families found highly unsatisfactory. Parents of most of these children withdrew them from the Monroe-Woodbury secular schools, citing "the panic, fear and trauma [the children] suffered in leaving their own communi-

ty and being with people whose ways were so different[."]
. . .

By 1989, only one child from Kiryas Joel was attending
Monroe-Woodbury's public schools; the village's other
handicapped children received privately funded special
services or went without. It was then that the New York
Legislature passed the statute at issue in this litigation,
which provided that the Village of Kiryas Joel "is constituted a separate school district, . . . and shall have and enjoy all the powers and duties of a union free school district. . . ." The statute thus empowered a locally elected
board of education to take such action as opening schools
and closing them, hiring teachers, prescribing textbooks,
establishing disciplinary rules, and raising property taxes
to fund operations. In signing the bill into law, Governor
Cuomo recognized that the residents of the new school
district were "all members of the same religious sect," but
said that the bill was "a good faith effort to solve th[e]
unique problem" associated with providing special education services to handicapped children in the village.

Although it enjoys plenary [broad] legal authority over
the elementary and secondary education of all school-aged
children in the village, the Kiryas Joel Village School District currently runs only a special education program for
handicapped children. The other village children have
stayed in their parochial schools, relying on the new
school district only for transportation, remedial education,
and health and welfare services. If any child without
handicap in Kiryas Joel were to seek a public-school education, the district would pay tuition to send the child into
Monroe-Woodbury or another school district nearby. Under like arrangements, several of the neighboring districts
send their handicapped Hasidic children into Kiryas Joel,

so that two thirds of the full-time students in the village's public school come from outside. In all, the new district serves just over forty full-time students, and two or three times that many parochial school students on a part-time basis.

Several months before the new district began operations, . . . [Louis Grumet et al.] . . . brought this action. . . . [T]he trial court ruled for [Grumet], finding . . . the statute . . . unconstitutional under both the National and State Constitutions.

A divided Appellate Division affirmed [upheld] on the ground that [the Kiryas Joel School District law] had the primary effect of advancing religion, in violation of both constitutions. . . . [T]he state Court of Appeals [also] affirmed. . . .

"A proper respect for both the Free Exercise and the Establishment Clauses compels the State to pursue a course of 'neutrality' toward religion," favoring neither one religion over others nor religious adherents collectively over nonadherents. . . . [T]he statute creating the Kiryas Joel Village School District departs from this constitutional command by delegating the State's discretionary authority over public schools to a group defined by its character as a religious community, in a legal and historical context that gives no assurance that governmental power has been or will be exercised neutrally.

. . . . The Establishment Clause problem presented by [the Kiryas Joel School District law is that] a State may not delegate its civic authority to a group chosen according to a religious criterion. Authority over public schools belongs to the State, and cannot be delegated to a local school district defined by the State in order to grant political control to a religious group....

It is, first, not dispositive [controlling] that the recipients of state power in this case are a group of religious individuals united by common doctrine, not the group's leaders or officers. Although some school district franchise is common to all voters, the State's manipulation of the franchise for this district limited it to Satmars, giving the sect exclusive control of the political subdivision. In the circumstances of this case, the difference between thus vesting state power in the members of a religious group as such instead of the officers of its sectarian organization is one of form, not substance. It is true that religious people (or groups of religious people) cannot be denied the opportunity to exercise the rights of citizens simply because of their religious affiliations or commitments, for such a disability would violate the right to religious free exercise, which the First Amendment guarantees as certainly as it bars any establishment....

Of course, [the Kiryas Joel School District law] delegates power not by express reference to the religious belief of the Satmar community, but to residents of the "territory of the village of Kiryas Joel." ... But our analysis does not end with the text of the statute at issue, and the context here persuades us that [the Kiryas Joel School District law] effectively identifies these recipients of governmental authority by reference to doctrinal adherence, even though it does not do so expressly. We find this to be the better view of the facts because of the way the boundary lines of the school district divide residents according to religious affiliation, under the terms of an unusual and special legislative act.

It is undisputed that those who negotiated the village boundaries when applying the general village incorporation statute drew them so as to exclude all but Satmars, and that the New York Legislature was well aware that the village remained exclusively Satmar in 1989 when it adopted [the Kiryas Joel School District law]. The significance of this fact to the state legislature is indicated by the further fact that carving out the village school district ran counter to customary districting practices in the State. Indeed, the trend in New York is not toward dividing school districts but toward consolidating them. The thousands of small common school districts laid out in the early nineteenth century have been combined and recombined, first into union free school districts and then into larger central school districts, until only a tenth as many remain today. Most of these cover several towns, many of them cross county boundaries, and only one remains precisely coterminus with an incorporated village. The object of the State's practice of consolidation is the creation of districts large enough to provide a comprehensive education at affordable cost, which is thought to require at least five hundred pupils for a combined junior-senior high school. The Kiryas Joel Village School District, in contrast, has only thirteen local, full-time students in all (even including out-of-area and part-time students leaves the number under two hundred), and in offering only special education and remedial programs it makes no pretense to be a full-service district.

The origin of the district in a special act of the legislature, rather than the State's general laws governing school district reorganization, is likewise anomalous. Although the legislature has established some twenty existing school districts by special act, all but one of these are districts in name only, having been designed to be run by private organizations serving institutionalized children. They have neither tax bases nor student populations of their own but serve children placed by other school districts or public agencies. The one school district petitioners point to that was formed by special act of the legislature to serve a whole community, as this one was, is a district formed for a new town, much larger and more heterogeneous than this village, being built on land that straddled two existing districts. Thus the Kiryas Joel Village School District is exceptional to the point of singularity, as the only district coming to our notice that the legislature carved from a single existing district to serve local residents. Clearly this district "cannot be seen as the fulfillment of [a village's] destiny as an independent governmental entity."

Because the district's creation ran uniquely counter to state practice, following the lines of a religious community where the customary and neutral principles would not have dictated the same result, we have good reasons to treat this district as the reflection of a religious criterion for identifying the recipients of civil authority. Not even the special needs of the children in this community can explain the legislature's unusual Act, for the State could have responded to the concerns of the Satmar parents without implicating the Establishment Clause .... We therefore find the legislature's Act to be substantially equivalent to defining a political subdivision and hence the qualification for its franchise by a religious test, resulting in a purposeful and forbidden "fusion of governmental and religious functions."

The fact that this school district was created by a special and unusual Act of the legislature also gives reason for concern whether the benefit received by the Satmar community is one that the legislature will provide equally to other religious (and nonreligious) groups. . . .

The fundamental source of constitutional concern here is that the legislature itself may fail to exercise governmental authority in a religiously neutral way. The anomalously case-specific nature of the legislature's exercise of state authority in creating this district for a religious community leaves the Court without any direct way to review such state action for the purpose of safeguarding a principle at the heart of the Establishment Clause, that government should not prefer one religion to another, or religion to irreligion. Because the religious community of Kiryas Joel did not receive its new governmental authority simply as one of many communities eligible for equal treatment under a general law, we have no assurance that the next similarly situated group seeking a school district of its own will receive one. . . . Nor can the historical context in this case furnish us with any reason to suppose that the Satmars are merely one in a series of communities receiving the benefit of special school district laws. Early on in the development of public education in New York, the State rejected highly localized school districts for New York City when they were promoted as a way to allow separate schooling for Roman Catholic children.

The general principle [is] that civil power must be exercised in a manner neutral to religion. . . . [W]e are forced to conclude that the State of New York has violated the Establishment Clause.

In finding that [the Kiryas Joel School District law] violates the requirement of governmental neutrality by extending the benefit of a special franchise, we do not deny that the Constitution allows the state to accommodate reli-

gious needs by alleviating special burdens. Our cases
leave no doubt that in commanding neutrality the Religion Clauses do not require the government to be obliv-
ious to impositions that legitimate exercises of state power
may place on religious belief and practice. Rather, there
is "ample room under the Establishment Clause for
'benevolent neutrality which will permit religious exercise
to exist without sponsorship and without interference.'"
"[G]overnment may (and sometimes must) accommodate
religious practices and . . . may do so without violating the
Establishment Clause." The fact that [the Kiryas Joel
School District law] facilitates the practice of religion is
not what renders it an unconstitutional establishment.

But accommodation is not a principle without limits, and
what [the Kiryas Joel School District] seek[s] is an adjust-
ment to the Satmars' religiously grounded preferences
that our cases do not countenance. Prior decisions have
allowed religious communities and institutions to pursue
their own interests free from governmental interference,
but we have never hinted that an otherwise unconstitutional delegation of political power to a religious group
could be saved as a religious accommodation. [The Kiryas
Joel School District's] proposed accommodation singles
out a particular religious sect for special treatment, and
whatever the limits of permissible legislative accommodations may be, it is clear that neutrality as among religions
must be honored.

This conclusion does not, however, bring the Satmar parents, the Monroe-Woodbury school district, or the State of
New York to the end of the road in seeking ways to re-
spond to the parents' concerns. . . . [T]here are several alternatives here for providing bilingual and bicultural special education to Satmar children. Such services can per-

fectly well be offered to village children through the
Monroe-Woodbury Central School District. Since the Satmars do not claim that separatism is religiously mandated,
their children may receive bilingual and bicultural instruction at a public school already run by the Monroe-
Woodbury district. Or if the educationally appropriate
offering by Monroe-Woodbury should turn out to be a
separate program of bilingual and bicultural education at
a neutral site near one of the village's parochial schools,
this Court has already made it clear that no Establishment
Clause difficulty would inhere in such a scheme, adminis-
tered in accordance with neutral principles that would not
necessarily confine special treatment to Satmars.

. . . . In this case we are clearly constrained to conclude
that the statute before us fails the test of neutrality. It
delegates a power this Court has said "ranks at the very
apex of the function of a State," to an electorate defined
by common religious belief and practice, in a manner that
fails to foreclose religious favoritism. It therefore crosses
the line from permissible accommodation to impermissible establishment. The judgment of the Court of Appeals
of the State of New York is accordingly affirmed.

THE U.S. CONSTITUTION

PREAMBLE

We the people of the United States, in order to form a more perfect union, establish justice, insure domestic tranquility, provide for the common defense, promote the general welfare, and secure the blessings of liberty to ourselves and our posterity, do ordain and establish this Constitution for the United States of America.

ARTICLE I

Section 1. All legislative powers herein granted shall be vested in a Congress of the United States, which shall consist of a Senate and House of Representatives.

Section 2. (1) The House of Representatives shall be composed of members chosen every second year by the people of several states, and the electors in each state shall have the qualifications requisite for electors of the most numerous branch of the State Legislature.

(2) No person shall be a Representative who shall not have attained to the age of twenty-five years, and been seven years a citizen of the United States, and who shall not, when elected, be an inhabitant of that state in which he shall be chosen.

(3) Representatives and direct taxes shall be apportioned among the several states which may be included within this union, according to their respective numbers, which shall be determined by adding to the whole number of free persons, including those bound to service for a term of years, and excluding Indians not taxed, three-fifths of all other persons. The actual enumeration shall be made

within three years after the first meeting of the Congress of the United States, and within every subsequent term of ten years, in such manner as they shall by law direct. The number of Representatives shall not exceed one for every thirty thousand, but each state shall have at least one Representative; and until such enumeration shall be made, the State of New Hampshire shall be entitled to choose three, Massachusetts eight, Rhode Island and Providence Plantations one, Connecticut five, New York six, New Jersey four, Pennsylvania eight, Delaware one, Maryland six, Virginia ten, North Carolina five, South Carolina five, and Georgia three.

(4) When vacancies happen in the representation from any state, the executive authority thereof shall issue Writs of Election to fill such vacancies.

(5) The House of Representatives shall choose their Speaker and other Officers; and shall have the sole power of impeachment.

Section 3. (1) The Senate of the United States shall be composed of two Senators from each state, chosen by the legislature thereof, for six years; and each Senator shall have one vote.

(2) Immediately after they shall be assembled in consequence of the first election, they shall be divided as equally as may be into three classes. The seats of the Senators of the first class shall be vacated at the expiration of the second year, of the second class at the expiration of the fourth year, and of the third class at the expiration of the sixth year, so that one-third may be chosen every second year; and if vacancies happen by resignation, or otherwise, during the recess of the legislature of any state, the execu-

tive thereof may make temporary appointments until the next meeting of the legislature, which shall then fill such vacancies.

(3) No person shall be a Senator who shall not have attained to the age of thirty years, and been nine years a citizen of the United States, and who shall not, when elected, be an inhabitant of that state for which he shall be chosen.

(4) The Vice President of the United States shall be President of the Senate, but shall have no vote, unless they be equally divided.

(5) The Senate shall choose their other Officers, and also a President pro tempore, in the absence of the Vice President, or when he shall exercise the Office of President of the United States.

(6) The Senate shall have the sole power to try all impeachments. When sitting for that purpose, they shall be on oath or affirmation. When the President of the United States is tried, the Chief Justice shall preside: and no person shall be convicted without the concurrence of two-thirds of the members present.

(7) Judgment in cases of impeachment shall not extend further than to removal from office, and disqualification to hold and enjoy any office of honor, trust, or profit under the United States: but the party convicted shall nevertheless be liable and subject to indictment, trial, judgment, and punishment, according to law.

Section 4. (1) The times, places and manner of holding elections for Senators and Representatives, shall be prescribed in each state by the legislature thereof; but the Congress may at any time by law make or alter such regulations, except as to the places of choosing Senators.

(2) The Congress shall assemble at least once in every year, and such meeting shall be on the first Monday in December, unless they shall by law appoint a different day.

Section 5. (1) Each House shall be the judge of the elections, returns, and qualifications of its own members, and a majority of each shall constitute a quorum to do business; but a smaller number may adjourn from day to day, and may be authorized to compel the attendance of absent members, in such manner, and under such penalties as each House may provide.

(2) Each House may determine the rules of its proceedings, punish its members for disorderly behavior, and, with the concurrence of two-thirds, expel a member.

(3) Each House shall keep a journal of its proceedings, and from time to time publish the same, excepting such parts as may in their judgment require secrecy; and the yeas and nays of the members of either House on any question shall, at the desire of one-fifth of those present, be entered on the journal.

(4) Neither House, during the Session of Congress, shall, without the consent of the other, adjourn for more than three days, nor to any other place than that in which the two Houses shall be sitting.

Section 6. (1) The Senators and Representatives shall receive a compensation for their services, to be ascertained by law, and paid out of the Treasury of the United States. They shall in all cases, except treason, felony and breach of the peace, be privileged from arrest during their attendance at the session of their respective Houses, and in going to and returning from the same; and for any speech or debate in either House, they shall not be questioned in any other place.

(2) No Senator or Representative shall, during the time for which he was elected, be appointed to any civil office under the authority of the United States, which shall have been created, or the emoluments whereof shall have been increased during such time and no person holding any office under the United States, shall be a member of either House during his continuance in office.

Section 7. (1) All bills for raising revenue shall originate in the House of Representatives; but the Senate may propose or concur with amendments as on other bills.

(2) Every bill which shall have passed the House of Representatives and the Senate, shall, before it become a law, be presented to the President of the United States; if he approve he shall sign it, but if not he shall return it, with his objections to the House in which it shall have originated, who shall enter the objections at large on their journal, and proceed to reconsider it. If after such reconsideration two-thirds of that House shall agree to pass the bill, it shall be sent together with the objections, to the other House, by which it shall likewise be reconsidered, and if approved by two-thirds of that House, it shall become a law. But in all such cases the votes of both Houses shall be determined by yeas and nays, and the names of the persons voting for and against the bill shall be entered on the journal of each House respectively. If any bill shall not

be returned by the President within ten days (Sundays excepted) after it shall have been presented to him, the same shall be a law, in like manner as if he had signed it, unless the Congress by their adjournment prevent its return in which case it shall not be a law.

(3) Every order, resolution, or vote, to which the concurrence of the Senate and House of Representatives may be necessary (except on a question of adjournment) shall be presented to the President of the United States; and before the same shall take effect, shall be approved by him, or being disapproved by him, shall be repassed by two-thirds of the Senate and House of Representatives, according to the rules and limitations prescribed in the case of a bill.

Section 8. (1) The Congress shall have the power to lay and collect taxes, duties, imposts and excises, to pay the debts and provide for the common defense and general welfare of the United States; but all duties, imposts and excises shall be uniform throughout the United States;

(2) To borrow money on the credit of the United States;

(3) To regulate commerce with foreign nations, and among the several states, and with the Indian Tribes;

(4) To establish an uniform Rule of Naturalization, and uniform laws on the subject of bankruptcies throughout the United States;

(5) To coin money, regulate the value thereof, and of foreign coin, and fix the standard of weights and measures;

(6) To provide for the punishment of counterfeiting the securities and current coin of the United States;

(7) To establish Post Offices and Post Roads;

(8) To promote the progress of science and useful arts, by securing for limited times to authors and inventors the exclusive right to their respective writings and discoveries;

(9) To constitute tribunals inferior to the Supreme Court;

(10) To define and punish piracies and felonies committed on the high seas, and offenses against the Law of Nations;

(11) To declare war, grant Letters of Marque and Reprisal, and make rules concerning captures on land and water;

(12) To raise and support armies, but no appropriation of money to that use shall be for a longer term than two years;

(13) To provide and maintain a Navy;

(14) To make rules for the government and regulation of the land and naval forces;

(15) To provide for calling forth the Militia to execute the laws of the Union, suppress insurrections and repel invasions;

(16) To provide for organizing, arming, and disciplining, the Militia, and for governing such part of them as may be employed in the service of the United States, reserving to the states respectively, the appointment of the Officers,

and the authority of training the Militia according to the discipline prescribed by Congress;

(17) To exercise exclusive legislation in all cases whatsoever, over such district (not exceeding ten miles square) as may, by cession of particular states, and the acceptance of Congress, become the Seat of the Government of the United States, and to exercise like authority over all places purchased by the consent of the legislature of the state in which the same shall be, for the erection of forts, magazines, arsenals, dockyards, and other needful buildings; and

(18) To make all laws which shall be necessary and proper for carrying into execution the foregoing powers, and all other powers vested by this Constitution in the Government of the United States, or in any Department or Officer thereof.

Section 9. (1) The migration or importation of such persons as any of the states now existing shall think proper to admit, shall not be prohibited by the Congress prior to the year one thousand eight hundred and eight, but a tax or duty may be imposed on such importation, not exceeding ten dollars for each person.

(2) The privilege of the Writ of Habeas Corpus shall not be suspended, unless when in cases of rebellion or invasion the public safety may require it.

(3) No Bill of Attainder or ex post facto law shall be passed.

(4) No capitation, or other direct, tax shall be laid, unless in proportion to the Census or enumeration herein before directed to be taken.

(5) No tax or duty shall be laid on articles exported from any state.

(6) No preference shall be given by any regulation of commerce or revenue to the ports of one state over those of another: nor shall vessels bound to, or from, one state be obliged to enter, clear, or pay duties in another.

(7) No money shall be drawn from the Treasury, but in consequence of appropriations made by law; and a regular statement and account of the receipts and expenditures of all public money shall be published from time to time.

(8) No title of nobility shall be granted by the United States: and no person holding any office of profit or trust under them, shall, without the consent of the Congress, accept of any present, emolument, office, or title, of any kind whatever, from any King, Prince, or foreign State.

Section 10. (1) No state shall enter into any treaty, alliance, or confederation; grant Letter of Marque and Reprisal; coin money; emit bills of credit; make any thing but gold and silver coin a tender in payment of debts; pass any Bill of Attainder, ex post facto law, or law impairing the obligation of contracts, or grant any title of nobility.

(2) No state shall, without the consent of the Congress, lay any imposts or duties on imports or exports, except what may be absolutely necessary for executing its inspection laws: and the net produce of all duties and imposts, laid by any state on imports or exports, shall be for the use of

the Treasury of the United States; and all such laws shall be subject to the revision and control of the Congress.

(3) No state shall, without the consent of Congress, lay any duty of tonnage, keep troops, or ships of war in time of peace, enter into any agreement or compact with another state, or with a foreign power, or engage in war, unless actually invaded, or in such imminent danger as will not admit of delay.

ARTICLE II

Section 1. (1) The executive power shall be vested in a President of the United States of America. He shall hold his office during the term of four years, and, together with the Vice President, chosen for the same term, be elected, as follows:

(2) Each state shall appoint, in such manner as the legislature thereof may direct, a number of electors, equal to the whole number of Senators and Representatives to which the state may be entitled in the Congress; but no Senator or Representative, or person holding an office of trust or profit under the United States, shall be appointed an Elector.

(3) The Electors shall meet in their respective states, and vote by ballot for two persons, of whom one at least shall not be an inhabitant of the same state with themselves. And they shall make a list of all the persons voted for, and of the number of votes for each; which list they shall sign and certify, and transmit sealed to the Seat of the Government of the United States, directed to the President of the Senate. The President of the Senate shall, in the presence of the Senate and House of Representatives,

open all the certificates, and the votes shall then be counted. The person having the greatest number of votes shall be the President, if such number be a majority of the whole number of Electors appointed; and if there be more than one who have such majority, and have an equal number of votes, then the House of Representatives shall immediately choose by ballot one of them for President; and if no person have a majority, then from the five highest on the list the said House shall in like manner choose the President. But in choosing the President, the votes shall be taken by states the representation from each state having one vote; a quorum for this purpose shall consist of a member or members from two-thirds of the states, and a majority of all the states shall be necessary to a choice. In every case, after the choice of the President, the person having the greater number of votes of the Electors shall be the Vice President. But if there should remain two or more who have equal votes, the Senate shall choose from them by ballot the Vice President.

(4) The Congress may determine the time of choosing the Electors, and the day on which they shall give their votes; which day shall be the same throughout the United States.

(5) No person except a natural born citizen, or a citizen of the United States, at the time of the adoption of this Constitution, shall be eligible to the Office of President; neither shall any person be eligible to that Office who shall not have attained to the age of thirty-five years, and been fourteen years a resident within the United States.

(6) In case of the removal of the President from Office, or of his death, resignation or inability to discharge the powers and duties of the said Office, the same shall devolve on the Vice President, and the Congress may by law

provide for the case of removal, death, resignation or inability, both of the President and Vice President, declaring what Officer shall then act as President, and such Officer shall act accordingly, until the disability be removed, or a President shall be elected.

(7) The President shall, at stated times, receive for his services, a compensation, which shall neither be increased nor diminished during the period for which he shall have been elected, and he shall not receive within that period any other emolument from the United States, or any of them.

(8) Before he enter on the execution of his Office, he shall take the following Oath or Affirmation: "I do solemnly swear (or affirm) that I will faithfully execute the Office of President of the United States, and will to the best of my ability, preserve, protect and defend the Constitution of the United States."

Section 2. (1) The President shall be Commander in Chief of the Army and Navy of the United States, and of the militia of the several states, when called into the actual service of the United States; he may require the opinion, in writing, of the principal Officer in each of the Executive Departments, upon any subject relating to the duties of their respective Offices, and he shall have power to grant reprieves and pardons for offenses against the United States, except in cases of impeachment.

(2) He shall have power, by and with the advice and consent of the Senate to make treaties, provided two-thirds of the Senators present concur; and he shall nominate, and by and with the advice and consent of the Senate, shall appoint Ambassadors, other public Ministers and Consuls,

Judges of the supreme Court, and all other Officers of the United States, whose appointments are not herein otherwise provided for, and which shall be established by law; but the Congress may by law vest the appointment of such inferior Officers, as they think proper, in the President alone, in the courts of law, or in the Heads of Departments.

(3) The President shall have power to fill up all vacancies that may happen during the recess of the Senate, by granting commissions which shall expire at the end of their next Session.

Section 3. He shall from time to time give to the Congress information on the State of the Union, and recommend to their consideration such measures as he shall judge necessary and expedient; he may, on extraordinary occasions, convene both Houses, or either of them, and in case of disagreement between them, with respect to the time of adjournment, he may adjourn them to such time as he shall think proper; he shall receive Ambassadors and other public Ministers; he shall take care that the laws be faithfully executed, and shall commission all the Officers of the United States.

Section 4. The President, Vice President and all civil Officers of the United States, shall be removed from office on impeachment for, and conviction of, treason, bribery, or other high crimes and misdemeanors.

ARTICLE III

Section 1. The judicial power of the United States, shall be vested in one supreme Court, and in such inferior courts as the Congress may from time to time ordain and establish. The Judges, both of the supreme and inferior courts, shall hold their Offices during good behaviour, and shall, at stated times, receive for their services a compensation, which shall not be diminished during their continuance in office.

Section 2. (1) The judicial power shall extend to all cases, in law and equity, arising under this Constitution, the laws of the United States, and treaties made, or which shall be made, under their authority; to all cases affecting Ambassadors, other public Ministers and Consuls; to all cases of admiralty and maritime jurisdiction; to controversies to which the United States shall be a party; to controversies between two or more states; between a state and citizens of another state; between citizens of different states; between citizens of the same state claiming lands under the grants of different states, and between a state, or the citizens thereof, and foreign states, citizens or subjects.

(2) In all cases affecting Ambassadors, other public Ministers and Consuls, and those in which a state shall be a party, the supreme Court shall have original jurisdiction. In all the other cases before mentioned, the supreme Court shall have appellate jurisdiction, both as to law and fact, with such exceptions, and under such regulations as the Congress shall make.

(3) The trial of all crimes, except in cases of impeachment, shall be by jury; and such trial shall be held in the state where the said crimes shall have been committed; but when not committed within any state, the trial shall be at such place or places as the Congress may by law have directed.

Section 3. (1) Treason against the United States, shall consist only in levying war against them, or, in adhering to their enemies, giving them aid and comfort. No person shall be convicted of treason unless on the testimony of two witnesses to the same overt act, or on confession in open Court.

(2) The Congress shall have power to declare the punishment of treason, but no Attainder of Treason shall work corruption of blood, or forfeiture except during the life of the person attainted.

ARTICLE IV

Section 1. Full faith and credit shall be given in each state to the public acts, records, and judicial proceedings of every other state. And the Congress may by general laws prescribe the manner in which such acts, records and proceedings shall be proved, and the effect thereof.

Section 2. (1) The citizens of each state shall be entitled to all privileges and immunities of citizens in the several states.

(2) A person charged in any state with treason, felony, or other crime, who shall flee from justice, and be found in another state, shall on demand of the executive authority of the state from which he fled, be delivered up, to be removed to the state having jurisdiction of the crime.

(3) No person held to service or labour in one state, under the laws thereof, escaping into another, shall, in consequence of any law or regulation therein, be discharged from such service or labour, but shall be delivered up on

claim of the party to whom such service or labour may be due.

Section 3. (1) New states may be admitted by the Congress into this Union; but no new state shall be formed or erected within the jurisdiction of any other state; nor any state be formed by the junction of two or more states, or parts of states, without the consent of the legislatures of the states concerned as well as of the Congress.

(2) The Congress shall have power to dispose of and make all needful rules and regulations respecting the territory or other property belonging to the United States; and nothing in this Constitution shall be so construed as to prejudice any claims of the United States, or of any particular state.

Section 4. The United States shall guarantee to every state in this Union a Republican form of government, and shall protect each of them against invasion; and on application of the Legislature, or of the Executive (when the Legislature cannot be convened) against domestic violence.

ARTICLE V

The Congress, whenever two-thirds of both Houses shall deem it necessary, shall propose amendments to this Constitution, or, on the application of the Legislatures of two-thirds of the several states, shall call a convention for proposing amendments, which, in either case, shall be valid to all intents and purposes, as part of this constitution, when ratified by the Legislatures of three-fourths of the several states, or by conventions in three-fourths thereof, as the one or the other mode of ratification may be proposed by the Congress; provided that no amendment which may be made prior to the year one thousand eight hundred and eight shall in any manner affect the first and fourth clauses in the Ninth Section of the first Article; and that no state, without its consent, shall be deprived of its equal suffrage in the Senate.

ARTICLE VI

(1) All debts contracted and engagements entered into, before the adoption of this Constitution shall be as valid against the United States under this Constitution, as under the Confederation.

(2) This Constitution, and the laws of the United States which shall be made in pursuance thereof; and all treaties made, or which shall be made, under the authority of the United States, shall be the supreme law of the land; and the Judges in every state shall be bound thereby, any thing in the Constitution or laws of any state to the contrary notwithstanding.

(3) The Senators and Representatives before mentioned, and the Members of the several State Legislatures, and all executive and judicial Officers, both of the United States and of the several states, shall be bound by oath or affirmation, to support this Constitution; but no religious test shall ever be required as a qualification to any Office or public trust under the United States.

ARTICLE VII

The ratification of the Conventions of nine states shall be sufficient for the establishment of this Constitution between the states so ratifying the same.

AMENDMENT I (1791)

Congress shall make no law respecting an establishment of religion, or prohibiting the free exercise thereof; or abridging the freedom of speech, or of the press; or the right of the people peaceably to assemble, and to petition the Government for a redress of grievances.

AMENDMENT II (1791)

A well regulated Militia, being necessary to the security of a free State, the right of the people to keep and bear arms, shall not be infringed.

AMENDMENT III (1791)

No soldier shall, in time of peace be quartered in any house, without the consent of the owner, nor in time of war, but in a manner to be prescribed by law.

AMENDMENT IV (1791)

The right of the people to be secure in their persons, houses, papers, and effects, against unreasonable searches and seizures, shall not be violated, and no warrants shall issue, but upon probable cause, supported by oath or affirmation, and particularly describing the place to be searched, and the persons or things to be seized.

AMENDMENT V (1791)

No person shall be held to answer for a capital, or otherwise infamous crime, unless on a presentment or indictment of a Grand Jury, except in cases arising in the land or naval forces, or in the Militia, when in actual service in time of war or public danger; nor shall any person be subject for the same offense to be twice put in jeopardy of life or limb; nor shall be compelled in any criminal case to be a witness against himself, nor be deprived of life, liberty, or property, without due process of law; nor shall private property be taken for public use, without just compensation.

AMENDMENT VI (1791)

In all criminal prosecutions, the accused shall enjoy the right to a speedy and public trial, by an impartial jury of the state and district wherein the crime shall have been committed, which district shall have been previously ascertained by law, and to be informed of the nature and cause of the accusation; to be confronted with the witnesses against him; to have compulsory process for obtaining witnesses in his favor, and to have the assistance of counsel for his defense.

AMENDMENT VII (1791)

In suits at common law, where the value in controversy shall exceed twenty dollars, the right of trial by jury shall be preserved, and no fact tried by jury, shall be otherwise re-examined in any Court of the United States, than according to the rules of the common law.

AMENDMENT VIII (1791)

Excessive bail shall not be required, nor excessive fines imposed, nor cruel and unusual punishments inflicted.

AMENDMENT IX (1791)

The enumeration in the Constitution, of certain rights, shall not be construed to deny or disparage others retained by the people.

AMENDMENT X (1791)

The powers not delegated to the United States by the Constitution, nor prohibited by it to the States, are reserved to the States respectively, or to the people.

AMENDMENT XI (1798)

The judicial power of the United States shall not be construed to extend to any suit in law or equity, commenced or prosecuted against one of the United States by citizens of another state, or by citizens or subjects of any foreign state.

AMENDMENT XII (1804)

The Electors shall meet in their respective states and vote by ballot for President and Vice-President, one of whom, at least, shall not be an inhabitant of the same state with themselves; they shall name in their ballots the person voted for as President, and in distinct ballots the person voted for as Vice-President, and they shall make distinct lists of all persons voted for as President, and of all persons voted for as Vice-President, and of the number of votes for each, which lists they shall sign and certify, and transmit sealed to the seat of the government of the United States, directed to the President of the Senate; the President of the Senate shall, in the presence of the Senate and House of Representatives, open all the certificates and the votes shall then be counted; the person having the greatest number of votes for President, shall be the President, if such number be a majority of the persons having the highest numbers not exceeding three on the list of those voted for as President, the House of Representatives shall choose immediately, by ballot, the President. But in choosing the President, the votes shall be taken by states, the representation from each state having one vote; a quorum for his purpose shall consist of a member or members from two-thirds of the states, and a majority of all the states shall be necessary to a choice. And if the House of Representatives shall not choose a President whenever the right of choice shall devolve upon them before the fourth day of March next following, then the Vice-President shall act as President, as in the case of the death or other constitutional disability of the President. The person having the greatest number of votes as Vice-President, shall be the Vice-President, if such number be a majority of the whole number of Electors appointed, and if no person have a majority, then from the two highest numbers on the list, the Senate shall choose the Vice-President; a quorum for the purpose shall consist of two-thirds of the whole number of Senators, and a majority of the whole number shall be necessary to a choice. But no person constitutionally ineligible to the office of President shall be eligible to that of Vice-President of the United States.

AMENDMENT XIII (1865)

Section 1. Neither slavery nor involuntary servitude, except as a punishment for crime whereof the party shall have been duly convicted, shall exist within the United States, or any place subject to their jurisdiction.

Section 2. Congress shall have power to enforce this article by appropriate legislation.

AMENDMENT XIV (1868)

Section 1. All persons born or naturalized in the United States, and subject to the jurisdiction thereof, are citizens of the United States and of the state wherein they reside. No state shall make or enforce any law which shall abridge the privileges or immunities of citizens of the United States; nor shall any state deprive any person of life, liberty, or property, without due process of law; nor deny to any person within its jurisdiction the equal protection of the laws.

Section 2. Representatives shall be apportioned among the several states according to their respective numbers, counting the whole number of persons in each State excluding Indians not taxed. But when the right to vote at any election for the choice of electors for President and Vice President of the United States, Representatives in Congress, the Executive and Judicial officers of a state, or the members of the Legislature thereof, is denied to any of the male inhabitants of such state, being twenty-one years of age, and citizens of the United States, or in any way abridged, except for participation in rebellion, or other crime, the basis of representation therein shall be reduced in the proportion which the number of such male citizens shall bear to the whole number of male citizens twenty-one years of age in such state.

Section 3. No person shall be a Senator or Representative in Congress, or elector of President and Vice President, or hold any office, civil or military, under the United States, or under any state, who having previously taken an oath, as a member of Congress, or as an officer of the United States, or as a member of any state legislature, or as an executive or judicial officer of any state, to support the Constitution of the United States, shall have engaged in insurrection or rebellion against the same, or given aid or comfort to the enemies thereof. But Congress may by a vote of two-thirds of each House, remove such disability.

Section 4. The validity of the public debt of the United States, authorized by law, including debts incurred for payment of pensions and bounties for services in suppressing insurrection or rebellion, shall not be questioned. But neither the United States nor any state shall assume or pay any debt or obligation incurred in aid of insurrection or rebellion against the United States, or any claim for the loss or emancipation of any slave; but all such debts, obligations and claims shall be held illegal and void.

Section 5. The Congress shall have power to enforce, by appropriate legislation, the provisions of this article.

AMENDMENT XV (1870)

Section 1. The right of citizens of the United States to vote shall not be denied or abridged by the United States or by any state on account of race, color, or previous condition of servitude.

Section 2. The Congress shall have power to enforce this article by appropriate legislation.

AMENDMENT XVI (1913)

The Congress shall have power to lay and collect taxes on income, from whatever source derived, without apportionment among the several states, and without regard to any census or enumeration.

AMENDMENT XVII (1913)

(1) The Senate of the United States shall be composed of two Senators from each state, elected by the people thereof, for six years; and each Senator shall have one vote. The electors in each State shall have the qualifications requisite for electors of the most numerous branch of the state legislatures.

(2) When vacancies happen in the representation of any state in the Senate, the executive authority of such state shall issue writs of election to fill such vacancies: *provided,* that the legislature of any state may empower the executive thereof to make temporary appointments until the people fill the vacancies by election as the legislature may direct.

(3) This amendment shall not be so construed as to affect the election or term of any Senator chosen before it becomes valid as part of the Constitution.

AMENDMENT XVIII (1919)

Section 1. After one year from the ratification of this article the manufacture, sale, or transportation of intoxicating liquors within, the importation thereof into, or the exportation thereof from the United States and all territory subject to the jurisdiction thereof for beverage purposes is hereby prohibited.

Section 2. The Congress and the several states shall have concurrent power to enforce this article by appropriate legislation.

Section 3. This article shall be inoperative unless it shall have been ratified as an amendment to the Constitution by the legislatures of the several states, as provided in the Constitution, within seven years from the date of the submission hereof to the states by the Congress.

AMENDMENT XIX (1920)

(1) The right of citizens of the United States to vote shall not be denied or abridged by the United States or by any state on account of sex.

(2) Congress shall have power to enforce this article by appropriate legislation.

AMENDMENT XX (1933)

Section 1. The terms of the President and Vice President shall end at noon on the 20th day of January, and the terms of Senators and Representatives at noon on the 3d day of January, of the years in which such terms would have ended if this article had not been ratified; and the terms of their successors shall then begin.

Section 2. The Congress shall assemble at least once in every year, and such meeting shall begin at noon on the 3d day of January, unless they shall by law appoint a different day.

Section 3. If, at the time fixed for the beginning of the term of the President, the President elect shall have died, the Vice President elect shall become President. If the President shall not have been chosen before the time fixed for the beginning of his term, or if the President elect shall have failed to qualify, then the Vice President elect shall act as President until a President shall have qualified; and the Congress may by law provide for the case wherein neither a President elect nor a Vice President elect shall have qualified, declaring who shall then act as President, or the manner in which one who is to act shall be selected, and such person shall act accordingly until a President or Vice President shall have qualified.

Section 4. The Congress may by law provide for the case of the death of any of the persons from whom the House of Representatives may choose a President whenever the right of choice shall have devolved upon them, and for the case of the death of any of the persons from whom the Senate may choose a Vice President whenever the right of choice shall have devolved upon them.

Section 5. Sections 1 and 2 shall take effect on the 15th day of October following the ratification of this article.

Section 6. This article shall be inoperative unless it shall have been ratified as an amendment to the Constitution by the legislatures of three-fourths of the several states within seven years from the date of its submission.

AMENDMENT XXI (1933)

Section 1. The eighteenth article of amendment to the Constitution of the United States is hereby repealed.

Section 2. The transportation or importation into any state, territory, or possession of the United States for delivery or use therein of intoxicating liquors, in violation of the laws thereof, is hereby prohibited.

Section 3. This article shall be inoperative unless it shall have been ratified as an amendment to the Constitution by conventions in the several states, as provided in the Constitution, within seven years from the date of the submission hereof to the states by the Congress.

AMENDMENT XXII (1951)

Section 1. No person shall be elected to the office of the President more than twice, and no person who has held the office of President, or acted as President, for more than two years of a term to which some other person was elected President shall be elected to the office of President more than once. But this Article shall not apply to any person holding the office of President when this Article was proposed by the Congress, and shall not prevent any person who may be holding the office of President, or acting as President, during the term within which this Article becomes operative from holding the office of President or acting as President during the remainder of such term.

Section 2. This article shall be inoperative unless it shall have been ratified as an amendment to the Constitution by the legislatures of three-fourths of the several states within seven years from the date of its submission to the states by the Congress.

AMENDMENT XXIII (1961)

Section 1. The District constituting the seat of Government of the United States shall appoint in such manner as the Congress may direct:

A number of electors of President and Vice President equal to the whole number of Senators and Representatives in Congress to which the District would be entitled if it were a state, but in no event more than the least populous state; they shall be in addition to those appointed by the states, but they shall be considered, for the purposes of the election of President and Vice President, to be electors appointed by a state; and they shall meet in the District and perform such duties as provided by the twelfth article of amendment.

Section 2. The Congress shall have power to enforce this article by appropriate legislation.

AMENDMENT XXIV (1964)

Section 1. The right of citizens of the United States to vote in any primary or other election for President or Vice President, for electors for President or Vice President, or for Senator or Representative in Congress, shall not be denied or abridged by the United States, or any state by reason of failure to pay any poll tax or other tax.

Section 2. The Congress shall have power to enforce this article by appropriate legislation.

AMENDMENT XXV (1967)

Section 1. In case of the removal of the President from office or of his death or resignation, the Vice President shall become President.

Section 2. Whenever there is a vacancy in the office of the Vice President, the President shall nominate a Vice President who shall take office upon confirmation by a majority vote of both Houses of Congress.

Section 3. Whenever the President transmits to the President pro tempore of the Senate and the Speaker of the House of Representatives his written declaration that he is unable to discharge the powers and duties of his office, and until he transmits to them a written declaration to the contrary, such powers and duties shall be discharged by the Vice President as Acting President.

Section 4. Whenever the Vice President and a majority of either the principal officers of the executive departments or of such other body as Congress may by law provide, transmit to the President pro tempore of the Senate and the Speaker of the House of Representatives their written declaration that the President is unable to discharge the powers and duties of his office, the Vice President shall immediately assume the powers and duties of the office as Acting President.

Thereafter, when the President transmits to the President pro tempore of the Senate and the Speaker of the House of Representatives his written declaration that no inability exists, he shall resume the powers and duties of his office unless the Vice President and a majority of either the principal officers of the executive department or of such other body as Congress may by law provide, transmit within four days to the President pro tempore of the Senate and the Speaker of the House of Representatives their written declaration that the President is unable to discharge the powers and duties of his office. Thereupon Congress shall decide the issue, assembling within forty-eight hours for that purpose if not in session. If the Congress, within twenty-one days after receipt of the latter written declaration, or, if Congress is not in session, within twenty-one days after Congress is required to assemble, determines by two-thirds vote of both Houses that the President is unable to discharge the power and duties of his office, the Vice President shall continue to discharge the same as Acting President; otherwise, the President shall resume the powers and duties of his office.

AMENDMENT XXVI (1971)

Section 1. The right of citizens of the United States, who are eighteen years of age or older, to vote shall not be denied or abridged by the United States or by any state on account of age.

Section 2. The Congress shall have power to enforce this article by appropriate legislation.

AMENDMENT XXVII (1992)

No law, varying the compensation for the services of the Senators and Representatives, shall take effect, until an election of Representatives shall have intervened.

BIBLIOGRAPHY

MORMON POLYGAMY

O'Dea, Thomas F. *The Mormons.* Chicago, IL: University of Chicago Press, 1957.

Thompson, Roger M. *The Mormon Church.* New York, NY: Hippocrene Books, 1993.

THE RIGHT TO ATTEND
A PAROCHIAL SCHOOL

Kommers, Donald P., and Michael J. Wahoske, Editors. *Freedom and Education: Pierce v. Society of Sisters Reconsidered.* Notre Dame, IN: Center for Civil Rights, 1978.

RELIGIOUS LIBERTY

Jehovah's Witnesses: Proclaimers of God's Kingdom. Brooklyn, NY: Watchtower Bible and Tract Society of New York, 1993.

Konvitz, Milton R. *Fundamental Liberties of a Free People: Religion, Speech, Press, Assembly.* Ithaca, NY: Cornell University Press, 1957.

Leahy, James E. *The First Amendment, 1791-1991: Two Hundred Years of Freedom.* Jefferson, NC: McFarland & Co., 1991.

Penton, M. James. *Apocalypse Delayed: The Story of Jehovah's Witnesses.* Buffalo, NY: University of Toronto Press, 1985.

Richards, David A.J. *Toleration and the Constitution.* New York, NY: Oxford University Press, 1986.

Wagman, Robert J. *The First Amendment Book.* New York, NY: World Almanac, 1991.

PUBLIC MONEY FOR RELIGIOUS PURPOSES

McBrien, Richard P. *Caesar's Coin: Religion and Politics in America.* New York, NY: Macmillan, 1987.

Miller, Glenn T. *Religious Liberty in America: History and Prospects.* Philadelphia, PA: Westminster Press, 1976.

EARLY RELEASE
FOR RELIGIOUS INSTRUCTION

Davis, Mary D. *Weekday Religious Instruction: Classes for Public School Pupils Conducted on Released School Time.* Washington, DC: U.S. Government Printing Office, 1933.

SCHOOL PRAYER

Fenwick, Lynda B. *Should the Children Pray? A Historical, Judicial, and Political Examination of Public School Prayer.* Waco, TX: Baylor University Press, 1989.

Menendez, Albert J. *School Prayer and Other Religious Issues in American Public Education: A Bibliography.* New York, NY: Garland, 1985.

BIBLE READING IN THE PUBLIC SCHOOLS

Dolbeare, Kenneth M., and Phillip E. Hammond. *The School Prayer Decisions: from Court Policy to Local Practice.* Chicago, IL: University of Chicago Press, 1971.

Murray, William J. *Let Us Pray: A Plea for Prayer in our Schools.* New York, NY: W. Morrow, 1995.

O'Hair, Madalyn Murray. *An Atheist Epic: The Complete Unexpurgated Story of How the Bible and Prayers Were Removed From the Public Schools of the United States.* Austin, TX: American Atheist Press, 1989.

Pfeffer, Leo. *Church, State and Freedom.* Boston, MA: Beacon Press, 1967.

Stokes, A.P., and Leo Pfeffer. *Church and State in the United States.* New York, NY: Harper & Row, 1964.

Turner, James. *Without God, Without Creed: The Origins of Unbelief in America.* Baltimore, MD: Johns Hopkins University Press, 1985.

THE "MONKEY" LAW

Berra, Tim M. *Evolution and the Myth of Creationism.* Stanford, CA: Stanford University Press, 1990.

Darwin, Charles. *The Origin of Species.* New York, NY: Literary Classics, 1900.

DeCamp, L. Sprague. *The Great Monkey Trial.* New York, NY: Doubleday, 1968.

Larson, Edward J. *Trial and Error: The American Controversy Over Creation and Evolution.* New York, NY: Oxford University Press, 1985.

McGowen, Tom. *The Great Monkey Trial: Science vs. Fundamentalism in America.* New York, NY: Franklin Watts, 1990.

Scopes, John T., and James Presley. *Center of the Storm: Memoirs of John T. Scopes.* New York, NY: Holt, Rinehart & Winston, 1967.

Zetterberg, J. Peter. *Evolution vs. Creationism.* Phoenix, AZ: The Oryx Press, 1983.

TAX EXEMPTION FOR CHURCH PROPERTY

Bradley, Gerard V. *Church-State Relationships in America.* New York, NY: Greenwood Press, 1987.

Gay, Kathlyn. *Church and State: Government and Religion in the United States.* Brookfield, CT: Millbrook Press, 1992.

Goldberg, George. *Church, State and the Constitution.* Washington, DC: Regnery Gateway, 1987.

TAXPAYER SUPPORT OF RELIGIOUS SCHOOLS

Public Funds and Parochial Schools. New York, NY: American Jewish Congress, 1973.

COMPULSORY EDUCATION OF THE AMISH

Good, Merle. *Who Are the Amish?* Intercourse, PA: Good Books, 1985.

Kraybill, Donald B. *The Riddle of Amish Culture.* Baltimore, MD: Johns Hopkins University Press, 1989.

THE "TEN COMMANDMENTS" ACT

Boles, Donald E. *The Bible, Religion, and the Public Schools.* Ames, IA: Iowa State University Press, 1963.

Frommer, Arthur. *The Bible and the Public Schools.* New York, NY: Frommer/Pasmantier Publishing Corp., 1963.

THE CRECHE CASE

Alley, Robert S., Editor. *The Supreme Court on Church and State.* New York, NY: Oxford University Press, 1988.

Kurland, Philip B. *Religion and the Law of Church and State and the Supreme Court.* Chicago, IL: Aldine Publishing Company, 1962.

Menendez, Albert J. *The December Wars: Religious Symbols and Ceremonies in the Public Square.* Buffalo, NY: Prometheus Books, 1993.

Miller, Robert T., and Ronald B. Flowers. *Toward Benevolent Neutrality: Church, State, and the Supreme Court.* Waco, TX: Markham Press Fund, 1992.

ISLAMIC PRAYERS IN PRISON

Farah, Caesar E. *Islam: Beliefs and Observances.* New York, NY: Barron's, 1987.

Renard, John. *In the Footsteps of Muhammed: Understanding the Islamic Experience.* New York, NY: Paulist Press, 1992.

DISTRIBUTION OF RELIGIOUS LITERATURE

Adams, Arlin M., and Charles J. Emmerich. *A Nation Dedicated to Religious Liberty: The Constitutional Heritage of the Religion Clauses.* Philadelphia, PA: University of Pennsylvania Press, 1990.

Frankel, Marvin E. *Faith and Freedom: Religious Liberty in America.* New York, NY: Hill & Wang, 1994.

PRAYERS AT GRADUATION

Alley, Robert S. *School Prayer: the Court, the Congress, and the First Amendment.* Buffalo, NY: Prometheus Books, 1984.

Kik, Jacob M. *The Supreme Court and Prayer in the Public School.* Philadelphia, PA: Presbyterian and Reformed Publishing Company, 1963.

RITUAL ANIMAL SACRIFICE

Canizares, Raul. *Walking With the Night: The Afro-Cuban World of Santeria.* Rochester, VT: Destiny Books, 1993.

Gonzalez-Wippler, Migene. *The Santeria Experience.* Englewood Cliffs, NJ: Prentice-Hall, 1982.

THE JEWISH SCHOOL DISTRICT

Harris, Lis. *Holy Days: The World of a Hasidic Family.* New York, NY: Summit Books, 1985.

Landau, David. *Piety and Power: The World of Jewish Fundamentalism.* New York, NY: Hill & Wang, 1993.

THE FIRST AMENDMENT
AND FREEDOM OF RELIGION

Alley, Robert S., Editor. *James Madison on Religious Liberty.* Buffalo, NY: Prometheus Books, 1985.

Eastland, Terry, Editor. *Religious Liberty in the Supreme Court: The Cases That Define the Debate Over Church and State.* Washington, DC: Ethics and Public Policy Center, 1993.

Flowers, Ronald B. *That Godless Court? Supreme Court Decisions on Church-State Relationships.* Louisville, KY: Westminster John Knox Press, 1994.

Goldwin, Robert A., and Art Kaufman, Editors. *How Does the Constitution Protect Religious Freedom?* Washington, DC: American Enterprise Institute for Public Policy Research, 1987.

Ivers, Gregg. *Lowering the Wall: Religion and the Supreme Court in the 1980s.* New York, NY: Anti-Defamation League, 1991.

Kramnick, Isaac, and R. Laurence Moore. *The Godless Constitution: The Case Against Religious Correctness.* New York, NY: Norton, 1996.

Levy, Leonard W. *The Establishment Clause: Religion and the First Amendment.* New York, NY: Macmillan, 1986.

Lynn, Barry W., Marc D. Stern, and Oliver S. Thomas. *The Right to Religious Liberty: The Basic ACLU Guide to Religious Rights.* Carbondale, IL: Southern Illinois University Press, 1995.

Marnell, William H. *The First Amendment: The History of Religious Freedom in America.* New York, NY: Doubleday, 1964.

Miller, William L. *The First Liberty: Religion and the American Republic.* New York, NY: Knopf, 1986.

Richards, David A.J. *Toleration and the Constitution.* New York, NY: Oxford University Press, 1986.

Weber, Paul J., Editor. *Equal Separation: Understanding the Religion Clauses of the First Amendment.* New York, NY: Greenwood Press, 1990.

Wills, Garry. *Under God: Religion and American Politics.* New York, NY: Simon & Schuster, 1990.

THE SUPREME COURT

Agresto, John. *The Supreme Court and Constitutional Democracy.* Ithaca, NY: Cornell University Press, 1984.

Cox, Archibald. *The Court and the Constitution.* New York, NY: Houghton-Mifflin, 1988.

Davis, Derck. *Original Intent: Chief Justice Rehnquist and the Course of American Church-State Relations.* Buffalo, NY: Prometheus Books, 1991.

Dumbauld, Edward. *The Bill of Rights and What It Means Today.* New York, NY: Greenwood Press, 1979.

Goode, Stephen. *The Controversial Court: Supreme Court Influences on American Life.* New York, NY: Messner, 1982.

Lawson, Don. *Landmark Supreme Court Cases.* Hillside: Enslow Publishers, Inc., 1987.

Rehnquist, William H. *The Supreme Court: How It Was, How It Is.* New York, NY: Morrow, 1987.

Woodward, Bob, and Scott Armstrong. *The Brethren: Inside the Supreme Court.* New York, NY: Simon & Schuster, 1979.

Yudof, Mark. *When Government Speaks: Politics, Law, and Government Expression in America.* Berkeley, CA: University of California Press, 1983.

INDEX

EXCELLENT BOOKS ORDER FORM

(Please xerox this form so it will be available to other readers.)

Please send

Copy(ies)

_____ of FREEDOM OF RELIGION DECISIONS @ $16.95 each
_____ of FREEDOM OF SPEECH DECISIONS @ $16.95 each
_____ of FREEDOM OF THE PRESS DECISIONS @ $16.95 each
_____ of LANDMARK DECISIONS @ $16.95 each
_____ of LANDMARK DECISIONS II @ $16.95 each
_____ of LANDMARK DECISIONS III @ $16.95 each
_____ of LANDMARK DECISIONS IV @ $16.95 each
_____ of LANDMARK DECISIONS V @ $16.95 each
_____ of ABORTION DECISIONS: THE 1970's @ $16.95 each
_____ of ABORTION DECISIONS: THE 1980's @ $16.95 each
_____ of ABORTION DECISIONS: THE 1990's @ $16.95 each
_____ of CIVIL RIGHTS DECISIONS: 19th CENTURY @ $16.95 ea.
_____ of CIVIL RIGHTS DECISIONS: 20th CENTURY @ $16.95 ea.
_____ of THE RAPE REFERENCE @ $16.95 each
_____ of THE MURDER REFERENCE @ $16.95 each
_____ of THE ADA HANDBOOK @ $16.95 each

Name: _____

Address: _____

City: _____ **State:** _____ **Zip:** _____

Add $1 per book for shipping and handling
California residents add sales tax

OUR GUARANTEE: Any Excellent Book may be returned at
any time for any reason and a full refund will be made.

Mail your check or money order to: Excellent Books,
Post Office Box 927105, San Diego, California 92192-7105
or call/fax (619) 598-5069